W9-ABA-089

An Uncompromising

ACTIVIST

An Uncompromising
ACTIVIST

MEMOIR OF AN IMMIGRANT, EDUCATOR, AND GRANDMOTHER

Nalini Juthani

iUniverse LLC
Bloomington

An Uncompromising Activist
Memoir of an Immigrant, Educator, and Grandmother

iUniverse books may be ordered through booksellers or by contacting:

iUniverse LLC
1663 Liberty Drive
Bloomington, IN 47403
www.iuniverse.com
1-800-Authors (1-800-288-4677)

ISBN: 978-1-4759-9872-6 (sc)
ISBN: 978-1-4759-9874-0 (hc)
ISBN: 978-1-4759-9873-3 (ebk)

Library of Congress Control Number: 2013912932

Printed in the United States of America

iUniverse rev. date: 07/31/2013

For My Husband
Viren
Our Children
Manisha, Kapila, Viral
and
Our Grandchildren

Table of Contents

List of Illustrations

Author's Note

Human beings have unique and interesting life experiences. We are all just ordinary people, living extra-ordinary lives. This memoir is written to share my experiences, to narrate what has touched me and inspired me in life. I have enjoyed the process of writing because it has given me an opportunity to walk down the memory lane and to reflect upon and relive some of these experiences.

In this book, I have created, refined, and retold the stories of the Ghevaria-Juthani families and friends who have inspired me and helped me to add new chapters in my life. Through descriptions of my experiences, I have emphasized my core values, positive moments of life, and ability to bounce back from difficult ones. These essays are accompanied by photographs, with a hope that coming generations of family members will build on them, continuing an intimate history of our family in the future.

We gratefully remember and honor those on whose shoulders we stand tall, having learned from their experiences and wisdom. It is now our mission to go forward with courage and confidence while preserving our core values that make us a special family.

Acknowledgements

I want to acknowledge the people whose names are mentioned in the stories. My late uncle Jay Gandhi, an author himself, inspired me to write this book. Although he did not live long enough to read this book, my gratitude goes to him for his support and encouragement.

I would like to thank my daughter Kapila who reviewed each story and helped me tell them in my own voice.

The most inspiring support came from my friend Bernice Gottlieb who listened to my stories with great interest and encouraged me to write a book.

My editor, Carol Barkin, offered me new insights into making this book interesting to people who do not know me.

Above all, the most personal and steadfast support came from my husband, Viren, my children Manisha, Kapila, and Viral. My grandchildren Ishani, Shaan, Kush, and Piya continue to amaze me every day with their creative thinking and loving talks. Kush and Piya ask me to tell them one story of my life every day when we are eating dinner together. I dedicate this book to them. Kush has urged me to also dedicate this book to the future additions to our precious grandchildren: children of Viral and Rupa.

Part I

The View Through an Immigrant's Eyes

1

From Those Who Have Been Given A Lot, A Lot Is Expected

In 2013, I spent a week at a medical camp in rural villages surrounding Rajkot, a small city in the state of Gujarat, in western India. I attended the camp with nine other doctors from the United States. The camp was organized by the Share and Care Foundation in the United States and the Sister Nivedita Foundation in Rajkot. We visited six schools, examined the students, gave them medicines and counseling for personal hygiene to prevent diseases, and met with teachers and parents to discuss ways to stay healthy.

I had never been to these very remote areas even when I lived in India for twenty-four years. I learned a lot about the people who live in rural India; their innocence, contentment, and curiosity touched me.

This is where I met a ten-year-old student, Sheetal, who was assigned by her teacher to be my assistant when I examined other students. She was incredibly observant and smart and kept a beautiful smile on her face. At the end of the second day, I asked her if she would like to come to the United States with me. She did not reply but stood lost in thought. When I asked if anything worried her, she smiled and said, "How did you know that?" She told me that her father had died in a motorbike accident when she was five years old; her two sisters were two years old and one month old at that time. Her mother became the breadwinner and started to work on a farm owned by her father and his brother.

When Sheetal was eight, her mother developed a serious toxic effect from a medicine and was hospitalized. Sheetal was terrified. Whenever she thinks about that episode even now, she worries; she is very aware that if something happened to her mother, she will be the caretaker of her two younger sisters. She said, "If I come with you to the United States, who will take care of my sisters?"

She sounded so mature at such a young age, and her story resonated with my own. My father passed suddenly from an abdominal hemorrhage, when I was five years old. My sister was just a newborn baby, and my mother became the breadwinner of our family. All through my growing-up years, I felt I had to take care of my family since there was no man to do it. But my life took a turn for the better because my grandparents gave us an opportunity to get education. In Rajkot, I reflected that educating girls like Sheetal will open up a whole new life for them. I decided to sponsor Sheetal's education, and that of her sisters, through high school.

When we had to leave the camp, I took pictures with Sheetal, and told her about my plan to educate all three of them one by one. She was tearful that we were leaving but said, "Foreigners who arrive here have to leave some day." She also said, "Maybe I will see you next year when you come to this camp again." I nodded.

This journey gave me an opportunity to examine how far I had come in life because I had an opportunity to become educated. I am delighted that the medical camp allowed me to meet smart girls like Sheetal and peek into their lives. My experience with Sheetal's family exemplifies my feeling that much has been given to me and now much is expected of me to give back.

2

The Adventure Begins

Virendra (Viren), age 29 in 1970 when Nalini first met him

Nalini, age 24 in 1970 when she first met Viren

I met Viren through common relatives. We clicked from our very first meeting. I admired his untraditional, independent thinking and his courage to be different. We were attracted to each other's ambitions. Like me, Viren had plans to move to America for further medical education. We had similar career goals, similar dreams, and similar family backgrounds, and we both had a sense of adventure. I agreed to marry Viren after our initial meeting, knowing that, in an arranged marriage, love would develop over time.

On March 29, 1970, Viren and I were engaged, with a plan to get married two months later. During those two months we spent every available minute together, getting to know each other and planning for our honeymoon and new life abroad.

Viren had signed a contract with a hospital in Highland Park, Michigan, to work as an internal medicine intern. Though I had finished medical school, I had not yet completed my internship. I was the first intern from Bombay University to be granted permission by the dean of the medical school to fulfill the remaining requirements of my internship year abroad.

Viren and I got married on May 31, 1970, in a traditional Bombay wedding. We had a short honeymoon in Ooty, a hill station in south India. We were still trying to know each other, but we had fallen in love and we had a wonderful time. One month after our wedding, on June 28, 1970, we left India for our adventure in the United States. Neither we nor our families knew that this adventure would continue for a lifetime, that America would be the place where we would fulfill our dreams, raise a family, and find a new home.

As we set off to America with borrowed money, the future was totally unknown to us. We had never traveled on an airplane and had never been away from home. We did not know anyone in Highland Park, Michigan.

Viren began work as soon as we arrived on July 1, 1970. Because he worked fifteen to twenty hours every day at the hospital, I took care of our day-to-day survival. We hardly had any time to spend together.

Each month, Viren brought his paycheck home and placed it in my hands. He did not ask where I was spending the money. One day I asked him if he worried that someday I could disappear with his hard-earned dollars. He responded without a moment's hesitation. He said that if I were to disappear with his checks, he would have so much more to cry about than the lost money. I was touched by his level of trust and loyalty. From that day on, I knew that together, Viren and I could overcome any obstacle that came our way.

For over thirty years, Viren and I have pursued our individual careers. My successful academic career was greatly enabled by Viren's emotional support and his willingness to share in the upbringing of our children.

One year, I was invited to give a commencement speech to the graduates of St. John's College in Queens, New York City. Many of those graduates were female immigrants from all over the world. During my speech, I reminded the graduates that the corollary to the famous saying is also true: "Behind every successful woman, there is always a man." I told the graduates that in my case, that man was my husband. I received loud applause from the audience; most of them were the spouses of these female graduates.

I migrated to the United States of America with three partners. One is my husband, Viren; two, my love for education and travel; and three, my Indian accent. I am happy to say that none of these partners have deserted me so far.

Nalini before the wedding ceremony on May 31, 1970

Nalini and Viren at their wedding reception
with Nalini's mother Sushila and sister Niru

Nalini and Viren during their honeymoon

Nalini preparing to leave home for the United States of America

At the airport, family and friends came to wish Nalini
and Viren "bon voyage"

Nalini and Viren in the United States of America 34 years later

3

A Lifetime Of Firsts

Viren with their first car, a Chevy Nova, in 1970

Cora Chatman, Nalini's first friend in America

Nalini and Viren's first house on 201 Ferndale Road
in Scarsdale, New York

"You've got to write about your experiences as an immigrant," friends and acquaintances have told me. They believe that these experiences have so much to convey about human resilience.

For me and Viren, life as immigrants in America involved numerous new and exciting experiences. Though some were eye-opening and others challenging, all of these "firsts" informed our knowledge of our new country and have given us cherished, and sometimes hilarious, memories to look back on.

My First American Friend

Arriving in Michigan in 1970, I began to learn new ways of life and soon realized how culturally different we were from native-born Americans.

Coming from India, where people have a range of brown-colored skin, I quickly understood that we were neither white nor black Americans. My real asset was that I could converse in English, and I did not hesitate to ask people for help, which I invariably received. Viren and I realized that because he was working such long hours, it would be very difficult for me to do the same at the same time. We decided that I would wait to start my training and would instead find paramedical jobs with fixed hours. During this time I was able to meet people of all colors and ethnicities and educate myself about American culture, which was totally new to us. I realized that my soul was peaceful in this new country. I was beginning to find my real self.

My first new friend in Highland Park was a black nurse named Cora Chatman. We worked together in the operating room at Highland Park Hospital, where I had gotten a job as a surgeon's assistant. She liked my innocence, but she was concerned that I was totally naïve.

Cora was my cultural ambassador, educator, and protector. She told me about the tensions between whites and blacks where we lived and worked. She and I watched the movie—"*Roots*"—together, and I learned the history of black Americans' experience of slavery, the civil war, and the civil rights movement.

Despite our differences, Cora and I had a lot in common. She had a master's degree in education; she spoke elegantly and was culturally sensitive. She had been raised by a single mother. She was independent-minded and determined to overcome all odds. I identified with her values, which bonded us for a lifetime. Later we visited her in California, where she had moved and subsequently married and had a child. We talked about child-rearing issues, and this time I was the experienced mentor, because I already had my first child, Manisha. As time flew by, we continued to talk regularly on the phone, and when Manisha got married, I invited Cora and her family. Cora went out and bought herself a saree, and all of them participated in the traditional wedding dances. We still exchange Christmas cards with summaries of all the year's events, and when we talk on the phone now, it is as if we were never apart.

Our First Car

Shortly after we arrived in Highland Park, Viren and I bought our first car, a teal Chevy Nova, for $2,500. We were in our twenties, had just moved to America, and were excited by the mere thought that we were going to be car owners. Only very wealthy people owned cars in India at that time, and no one in our families had ever owned a car.

We had already taken the written exam for a driver's license. We were not required to take a driving test because we had gotten international driver's licenses in Bombay before we left. However, we had never driven a car with power steering and power brakes, nor had we ever driven on the right side of the street (India uses the British system in which people drive on the left side of the street). So it was quite an adventure for us to buy a car and just drive away.

Our new car gave us the freedom to better explore our new country. We spent many years traveling, learning, and making memories in our beloved teal Chevy Nova.

My First Job in New York

After Viren completed a year of internship, we moved from Michigan to New York City. I worked at various paramedical jobs while Viren completed his final two years of training as a resident in internal medicine. My first job in New York was as a surgeon's assistant in an abortion clinic in Manhattan's Union Square. I had found it through an employment agency. In addition to assisting the obstetrician, I enjoyed talking to the women about their reasons for getting an abortion.

The women who came to the clinic were of all cultures; some of them were immigrants, some were from other parts of the United States. I noticed that none of them came with a family member or the father of the fetus. Most of them looked sad, and many expressed tremendous guilt. They felt comfortable talking to me, although I was not a trained counselor.

One morning, I arrived at work as usual, only to find that the place was empty. The owner of the store next door told me that the place had been busted during the night because it was an illegal operation. I was very confused. *Wow, I was a new immigrant working for an illegal operation!* Cora had been right to think I was naïve. I later learned that at that time, abortion was illegal in New York and most other states as well. This explained why the women had come from far and wide and usually came by themselves.

I learned more about these women and the cultural norms of the United States than they learned from me. Providing an empathetic ear and some common-sense counseling was one of the experiences that sparked my interest in specializing in psychiatry.

Our First House

From 1970 through 1978, we lived in three apartments: one in Highland Park, Michigan, and two in Upper Manhattan. Then, after being in this country for eight years, we were finally able to fulfill our American Dream of owning our first house.

In 1977, I began my final year of residency training in psychiatry, and Viren had started to work as an attending physician. We were financially stable, with enough savings for a down payment. Our older daughter, Manisha, was five years old, and I was expecting our second child. It was the right time to look for a house, so that Manisha could start her formal education in a public school.

We wanted to live within half an hour from the hospitals in the Bronx where we both worked. We had searched the lists of highly acclaimed public schools; Westchester County seemed to be the right place to look. We decided to concentrate on looking in Scarsdale. Our goal was to find a house that was ten to fifteen years old, with central air-conditioning, located on one-half acre of land, in the price range of $125,000-$150,000.

We began to look for a house in late summer to early fall of 1977. I was to finish my residency in June 1978, the same month that our second child was due. We wanted to close on the house by March. With this plan in mind, we contacted a real estate agency and started looking at houses in the Scarsdale area. Our real estate agent was a friendly and patient lady. We saw eighty houses in Scarsdale with her. None of these houses fit the bill, and our contract with her came to an end.

Winter was fast approaching. We knew that it would be impossible to look for houses in the winter, and so we were not likely to close on a house by March 1978 as we had planned. We were disheartened.

On the first Sunday in December 1977, I was reading the real estate section of the *New York Times.* A house in Edgemont (next to Scarsdale) was listed by the owner. We called him immediately, and he told us that someone had seen the house early that morning and had made an offer. I was very disappointed because without even seeing the house, I knew I would have liked it. The owner took our phone number and promised to contact us if the deal did not go through. Though we had lost hope, we went to see the house from the outside and wished that it could be ours.

Four weeks passed. We had stopped looking at houses. Then, one Sunday, the kind gentleman in Edgemont called us and said that the people who had made an offer on the house were not able to obtain a mortgage. He invited us to come and see the house as he was planning to list it again in the *New York Times.*

Excitedly, we set off. The house was twenty-six years old, though every room was renovated. It did not have central air-conditioning, though it did have individual units

24

in each room. It was sitting on one-third, not one-half, of an acre of land. This house did not meet any of our criteria for our dream house. However, Viren and I both fell in love with it. It was meant for us. We did not want to leave. We visited each room several times and visualized raising our family in this house. The owner allowed us to use his family room for a private discussion.

Viren and I did not always see eye-to-eye on every major issue, but this was a unanimous decision. We loved the house, even though it did not fulfill any of the requirements we had set up six months earlier. We made an offer, and the owner accepted it on the spot. We were delighted and grateful.

We closed on the house at 201 Ferndale Road in Edgemont in March 1978, just as we had planned. This was our first house: the home in which we were able to fulfill our dreams of raising a family.

4

Establishing An Identity

Manisha's preschool friends at New Rochelle Academy

When we came to America, we quickly became immersed in a completely different society from the one in which we had been raised. We were happy to learn about American society and culture and were quickly able to join the "melting pot" of New York. Since we were steeped in the culture of our birth, we did not feel any need to maintain our cultural heritage. It was only through the eyes and experiences of our first daughter, Manisha, that we realized the need to develop a cultural, racial, ethnic and religious identity within the "salad bowl" of American society. Because really, America is not a melting pot, it is more like a salad bowl or a cultural mosaic in which different groups retain their uniqueness while serving a common goal.

After our year in Michigan, we lived in New York City and worked with people of many different nationalities and cultures. We had no difficulty merging in this diverse group. We had African-American colleagues, European-American colleagues, and a few Asian-American colleagues as well. The majority of our friends were immigrants. We all were different and our racial differences were never a topic of discussion, though it was clear to Viren and me that the color of one's skin played a big role in American society.

While we were living in New York City, Manisha spent three years in preschool at New Rochelle Academy. Although it was a very diverse preschool, Manisha was the only Indian child in her class. But she did not seem to be bothered by that. She always came home happy. Before she learned the other kids' names, Manisha would talk about playing with her "dark brown" friend or doing a craft project with her "light brown" friend. At such an early age, I did not want to corrupt her tender mind with the notion of racial-color differences.

Then, in 1978, we moved to Edgemont, a small community in Westchester County, New York, known to have great schools. Edgemont does not have a postal address; therefore our postal address is Scarsdale. Edgemont has its own schools and it is governed by the town of Greenburgh. We knew that three Indian families lived in Edgemont. But they were just acquaintances.

Moving to Edgemont was somewhat of a culture shock for us. Most of the families were Caucasians who followed Jewish or Catholic religions. There were no other people of color in Greenville school at that time. We moved into our new house on March 28, 1978, and enrolled Manisha in first grade for the fall at Greenville Elementary School. We felt anxiety about whether she would be accepted by her classmates and teachers in this new town. Our anxiety was based on our differences. We were people of color who looked different, we ate vegetarian food, we were born in the Hindu religion, we were not familiar with the American school system, and we were not familiar with the sports culture of the United States. During the summer before Manisha started at Greenville, we walked around the school, played in the playground, and chatted with other mothers and children we met there.

Then the school year began. Manisha's new class was not made up of children who ranged in color from "light brown" to "dark brown" like those at New Rochelle Academy. To our surprise, she came home after her first day of school and proclaimed that in this school, all of her friends were "light brown" and that she was the only "medium brown" kid. We were surprised that she was so aware of her difference.

I shared this story with one of my neighbors, May, who was an older woman, almost my mother's age. She was Jewish, and she told me that when she had moved to Edgemont many years before, there had been a small pond where our house now stood. That pond had been a dividing line. Christian families lived on one side of the pond, and Jewish families had gradually begun to move in on the other side. The Christian people had not quickly accepted their new Jewish neighbors.

May told me that anytime a new group of people moved into the neighborhood, there was an adjustment period on both sides. But she advised me to continue being friendly and to have a thick skin. She told me, "People feel insecure when they don't know you. Try to share stories about your background, tell them that you both are doctors, and soon they will be comfortable with you." She also told me to let my daughter adapt in her own way, as long as she was comfortable with the other children. In time, Manisha came to accept that she was different but she was comfortable with her friends.

One day, Manisha told me that the best part of the school day was lunchtime. We are vegetarians and had raised Manisha to be vegetarian, based on our religious and spiritual belief that all souls are equal and we should not kill animals for the mere pleasure of eating meat. Although as a child I ate my lunch with my best friend, a Muslim who ate meat, I had accepted that difference between us. In my school in India, many of my classmates ate non-vegetarian food and many were vegetarians. However, no one in Manisha's class was vegetarian, which concerned me. We explained to her our rationale for being vegetarian. She asked several questions, but it seemed to me that she had understood our reasons for this choice. To overcome my anxiety, I started to volunteer as a lunch mom, one day a week, to watch what she did during lunchtime. I was surprised to see that she had made friends; she ate lunch with them and played with them. It seemed that I had been more anxious than she was, my anxiety based on the fact that we were different and in the minority in the community where we lived.

Manisha loved to have play dates. One day, she returned from school rather upset that she could not have a play date that day because Christine had to attend Bible school and Rachel had to attend Hebrew school. Although she did not know the significance of these schools, she did know that these were activities she was not enrolled in. She asked us at dinnertime, "Why don't I go to any of these schools?"

My husband and I looked at each other; this was a profound question. We explained to her that we were Hindus and that, to our knowledge, no Hindu school was available for children nearby. Boldly, she said, "We can start one, can't we?" Neither of us responded to her question, but the seed was planted in our minds.

Viren and I were first-generation immigrants, both doctors who needed further training in our respective specialties. We had wanted to have a family, buy a house, and make a living. We were succeeding in achieving these goals but had not thought beyond them.

Although we both were born Hindus, we were not observant Hindus. We knew all of the traditions and had celebrated festivals with our families when we were in India, but by no means had we mastered the Hindu scriptures. In America, we did not have any family with whom we could celebrate our festivals and continue our traditions. There was one Hindu temple under construction in Queens at that time. Manisha's thoughtful question about whether we could start our own Hindu school continued to haunt us. Some time passed. We now had our second daughter, Kapila. Giving our children some religious identity began to occupy our minds. We had no idea how to start a religious school and, if we did, we didn't know who else would enroll their kids. We knew some Hindu families in Queens and Long Island, but we hardly knew any in Westchester County.

We learned that in Queens, some religious classes for adults were given once a week. We started to drive to Queens with the children every Friday night to attend those classes. Some of the attendees realized that there was certainly a need for our children to develop a Hindu identity. We gathered the scriptures from India and asked for their translation in English and Gujarati (our native language).

None of us parents knew enough about the scriptures to provide religious instruction to our children. However, after many discussions between parents on what to teach and how to teach children, my friend and I volunteered to take on this challenge. Our husbands and other parents who attended the classes supported us all the way. They were delighted that we were willing to take on such an important project. We began by teaching prayers and telling religious stories, and we gradually introduced scripture through the stories.

Eventually, word got out that we were conducting these classes in Queens, and people in Westchester County urged us to start classes in Westchester. By this time many more Indian families had moved to Westchester County and we had become involved socially with them. The principal at Manisha's school, with our permission, gave many of those who were moving to Scarsdale our address so that they could contact us with any questions about the school and community. We started children's classes in our house. Manisha was delighted. She told her friends at school that a Hindu religious school had started, with her mom as the teacher, and that all her new friends looked like her, "medium brown."

This became our Sunday morning activity. The task of studying the scriptures and translating their meaning into English was not easy, but it was indeed exciting. Manisha looked forward to Sunday mornings. She knew that Mommy had to study before the class began. As more students joined us, we started renting a school gym for two hours every Sunday morning to hold our class.

As time went on, more families began to come to our Hindu school with their kids. My daughter had never seen so many children who looked like her and whose parents looked like her parents. This was the beginning of my ongoing discussion with Manisha about developing an identity that takes into account our race, ethnicity, culture, values, and religion. Although our discussions when she was five were very basic, Manisha and I continue to discuss cultural issues even today. I realized that my initial desire as an immigrant was to be accepted, and the way acceptance was possible was to melt into the American melting pot. As I became more aware of what I was gaining and what I was losing by melting into the melting pot, I retreated because of my fear that my identity as an Indian would also melt away. I wanted to preserve my cultural values and traditions and develop my unique identity in a new country. This required endorsing separation of cultures and ethnicities and taking the best of both cultures.

After coming to America in 1970, I had realized that I was not white, black or Hispanic. Although we were lumped in a racial category called Asian, I could not relate to being in any way close to Chinese, Japanese, Filipino, Cambodian, Korean, Laotian, Vietnamese, etc. A decade or two later, the racial identity called South Asian emerged. It was created by the next generation (children of first-generation immigrants) and included Indian, Pakistani, Sri Lankan, and Bangladeshi.

My colleagues used to say that we are really Caucasians tanned in the sun for over a thousand years. However, I felt that my racial-ethnic identity in the United States was in a state of flux, evolving from being an Indian to a South Asian American to an American of Indian origin.

I discussed these issues with my professional colleagues and friends who were struggling with similar issues. I read about earlier immigrants to the United States who had gone through similar struggles. Most immigrants from European countries migrated to escape adversities or as refugees. They had issues of survival when they left their country of origin. They were in some respects willing to give up the past and start a new future. In my case, however, we had come to enhance our professional lives and to have better opportunities in the United States. We had a past with which we kept constant contact. We visited India very frequently; we had taken Manisha to India twice before she was five years old. It was becoming clear to me that if I were to have the best of both worlds (Indian and American), my struggles would be infinite. We would be challenged at every step as we raised our American-born children. I studied firsthand a lot of these issues through Manisha's experiences as she progressed from elementary school to high school. Although at every phase it was a challenge to reexamine our cultural values, I became more confident that we could raise children with an integrated identity who would eventually be comfortable in society with their differences and similarities. Even today, we continue to discuss the differences and similarities that bring human beings together and set them apart.

Part II

The Building Blocks of a Life

5

Best Friends

Nalini and Amta in their teenage years

Lifelong friends Nalini and Amta

I grew up in a large metropolitan city, Mumbai, India. During the 1950s and 1960s, the caste system was not as prevalent in large cosmopolitan cities and especially in my family as it was in rural areas. However, people were recognized and classified based on where their ancestors had emerged from and on their religious background. I was, therefore, a Gujarati (my ancestors emerged from a state called Gujarat in India). My family spoke *Gujarati* in the house and we followed the Hindu religion. We lived in a highly diverse community in which people had come from various parts of India and therefore spoke a number of different Indian languages. Another difference in this neighborhood was the kind of food people ate. There were vegetarians and non-vegetarians. The amazing thing was that people lived in harmony for decades but they socialized and arranged marriages only with their own kind.

I went to a private all-girls school; my grandfather and father had both been attorneys, and higher education was expected in my family. Children from many different backgrounds were enrolled in my school, and all subjects were taught in English. It was in this school that I met my childhood best girlfriend, Amta. In India girls had best girlfriends and boys had best boyfriends; it was socially frowned upon if a girl and a boy were best friends and went out together in public. Gay and lesbian categories were unknown in those days. It was not uncommon to see grown men hold hands when they were out and this was also true for women.

Amta and I enjoyed each other's company outside of school as well. As we became teenagers, we went shopping on Saturdays and to the movies on Sundays. We met outside somewhere and never talked about going to each other's house. I am of the Hindu faith and Amta is of the Muslim faith, but we never talked about our religions.

Amta ate non-vegetarian food and I ate vegetarian food. When we ate in restaurants together, Amta never ordered non-vegetarian food, but when we ate lunch in school together, she ate her home food and I ate mine. My other girlfriends would not sit next to girls who ate non-vegetarian lunch, so there were two groups of girls sitting away from each other at lunchtime. I was never tempted to try meat from Amta's lunch nor did my conviction not to eat meat weaken. I respected Amta's eating preference and did not feel a need to judge her based on our differences.

We were in high school and our teacher assigned a project to do at home. Two students had to pair up and do the project together. Amta and I paired up, but we really had not considered that it meant going to each other's house and spending several hours together, which might lead to our families finding out that we were Hindu-Muslim best friends.

I arrived at her house. The neighborhood was very different from mine. Many women wore *burkhas*, which are long black gowns with faces covered by a netted mask. However, Amta's female relatives dressed in outfits similar to what my family wore. Amta explained that they wore long black gowns only when they went to the mosque for prayers. Her mother, father, and sister welcomed me with open arms; they did not offer anything to eat but gave me a soft drink, which I accepted with gratitude. As I continued to visit Amta's home to complete our project, her two brothers became friendlier with me. I learned a lot about how Muslims lived and understood their ways of life firsthand. I learned that many Muslims prayed five times a day, but Amta's family prayed in the morning and at night. They ate as a group from a large platter in which food was arranged in the center and each of them took as much as they wanted on their side. They showed gratitude to God by saying that all good things were happening to them because that was God's will.

Now it was time for Amta to come to my house. My family, however, reacted very differently to the idea. They told me stories of Muslims who helped kill Hindus during the independence riot of 1946 in India. They told me that friendship was no barrier to such killings. I did not understand why events that had occurred in 1940s, two decades ago were remembered so vividly by my family members.

When Amta arrived at my home, she received a lukewarm welcome from my mother. We finished our project, and I asked my mother if we could eat together. She reluctantly agreed. Hindus did not feel comfortable eating with a Muslim and a non-vegetarian, and of course my family did not know that Amta and I ate our lunches sitting side by side in school every day. I had kept that a secret, probably because I knew my family would be unhappy about it.

Amta and I talked about these experiences, but our friendship was not shaken. We learned about each other's religious values and discovered that they seemed very similar. We respected each other's differences as well. It is now over fifty years that our friendship has remained steadfast. We live 10,000 miles away from each other and there was a period in our lives when there was no easy telephone communication. When we called each other once a year, the first thing we said to each other was, "Everything is all right, I am just calling to hear your voice."

I have lived in the United States for almost forty-five years. When I visit India once a year, Amta is the first one to welcome me "home," to meet me at the airport and say

"I have missed you so much," and when I leave she is the last one to say goodbye.

When we separate, we both become emotional but hold back our tears. I say, "Goodbye until we meet again," and she says "Goodbye, *Insha'Allah*," meaning God *(Allah)* willing.

6

Growing Up as a Woman in India

Nalini with her mother, Sushila, and father, Kantilal

When I was just a few years old, I met a five-year-old girl named Nayna on a family vacation. I liked her very much and I decided that my name should also be Nayna. I told my family that I would only respond to the name Nayna from then on. And so, although my birth name was Nalini, I was called Nayna by everyone who knew me, until I was married, over twenty years later. How many people have named them?

From that moment on, my family knew that I would grow up to be "different" from most people. I decided who I was going to be (both in name and in character), regardless of what others expected of me, from a very early age. However, I often struggled to reconcile who I was with the social norms around me.

The single formational event of my childhood, which shaped the way I viewed myself, my family, and my society, was the untimely death of my beloved father, Kantilal Ghevaria. He passed away after a twenty-four-hour abdominal hemorrhage in 1951 when I was five years old. As he lay dying in the hospital, he told his family that he wanted to feed me peaches (my favorite fruit)—that act of love has stayed with me throughout my life. When my father died, he was only twenty-seven years old and my mother, Sushila Ghevaria, who was then three months pregnant, was twenty-five.

My father had graduated from law school, and he was scheduled to represent his first client in court one day after his death. He had purchased a life insurance policy, which was supposed to take effect one week after his death. My mother felt that all of these events demonstrated that she was meant to survive and raise her family as a single parent, though she had been left without many resources.

In those days, it was considered unacceptable for a widowed woman to marry again or to live alone without a husband. My mother's parents invited us to live with them. I grew up in the home of my maternal grandparents and my maternal uncle, who became my friend, my role model, and my father figure.

Although my grandparents were relatively wealthy, my mother never failed to remind me that I was the daughter of a widowed mother, who could not afford luxury for her children. She saw herself as a victim of her circumstances. She often sang a Hindi song, whose lyrics can be loosely translated as "When every household celebrated Diwali, a festival of lights, she had nothing but darkness in her mind, body and soul."

I vividly remember one crisp morning about six months after my father died, when my grandmother told me that my mother was going to the hospital to bring me a baby brother. All of my relatives hoped and dreamed that God would give my mother a son, who would take care of his mother and sister when he grew up. I was six years old and did not quite understand the difference between having a brother or a sister. Of course, my pessimistic mother had told me that she knew she would deliver a baby girl. Sadly, my sister's birth was a somber event for my family. Niru, was a quiet and cute little girl. My mother became preoccupied with raising her, so I turned to my grandmother and sought comfort in her.

Until I was ten years old, my mother and other well-wishers told me that my father was abroad getting a higher law degree. They wanted to protect me from the trauma of this monumental loss. As a child, I needed to believe that he would return one day. But when his death really sank into my heart and soul, I was overcome by a deep sense of loss and hurt.

I deeply experienced the loss of my father at every stage of my life. I cried easily when I thought of him. I looked to his memory and his spirit to help me choose the right path. My family reminded me that I looked like him and articulated my thoughts just as he had. When I expressed my convictions about anything, they would say, "There is no point in arguing with her because she has her father's genes."

Throughout my adolescence, I searched for the cause of my father's death, but to no avail. No doctors could provide a comprehensible explanation because he had been so young, with no history of alcoholism, peptic ulcers, or any bleeding disorders. However, my search for the cause of my father's death led me to develop an interest in medicine. In high school, my class was asked to write an essay on the topic "Who do I want to be when I grow up?" The main point of my essay was that I wanted to become a physician to be able to save the life of another little girl's father, so that she would never have to experience what I had.

The loss of my father stayed unresolved for me into my early adult years. As an adolescent, I experienced significantly more emotional turbulence than most adolescents. I questioned everything in my life, as well as the society around me.

An important question for me was whether I would be able to fulfill my family's expectations. Throughout my childhood and adolescence, my maternal grandfather gave me mixed messages about the role he expected me to fill. On the one hand, since there was no man in my nuclear family, I would have to pursue an education and become a professional woman so that I could be the breadwinner for my mother and younger sister, a role traditionally reserved for a son. On the other hand, I was also supposed to have an arranged marriage and bear children, as expected of every daughter.

This led me to further question the underlying societal belief system and traditions upon which my family based their expectations. Although India was one of the first countries in the world to elect a woman as prime minister, Indians generally have had a very limited view of a woman's role in society. When I was growing up in the 1960s, a woman's primary role in my community was that of a homemaker, a wife, and a mother. Therefore, the primary objective for any girl's family was to find her an appropriate husband, allowing her to fulfill this role. Having a career and working outside of the home was significantly frowned upon. People feared that if a daughter was educated, her matrimonial opportunities would become limited, especially in communities like mine where few men pursued higher education; in most arranged marriages, the woman was younger and less well educated than the man. I felt, though I could not express, the difficulty of fulfilling both of these conflicting expectations my family held for me.

I resented that my culture treated women as property. A woman followed her father's wishes as a little girl, then her husband's after marriage, and then her son's until she died. I promised myself that I would never be one of those women. Watching my mother, I despised the fact that she constantly played the role of a victim. I felt outraged that women who did not have husbands or sons, like my mother, felt victimized and refused to try to overcome the obstacles put in their path. I vowed never to give in to feelings of victimization myself.

Finally, I also questioned my society's emphasis on skin color. Although people of Indian origin range in skin color from light brown to dark brown, fair skin is highly valued over dark skin. Fair skin is associated with beauty, wealth, and social status. Having darker skin greatly hurt a woman's marital prospects. My family felt that since I was a dark-skinned woman (though my children now insist that that assessment was not accurate); I would have a better chance of finding a good husband if I pursued a profession. I resented the fact that society would judge me purely on my skin color, rather than on my character, my intelligence, or even my actual facial features.

As I questioned the society around me, I gradually became an uncompromising activist for the principles about which I felt strongly. For example, I believed that I should be able to express my feelings and articulate my thoughts freely; that an appropriate spouse for me would be an independent provider rather than someone who simply took over a family business; and that an appropriate spouse need not necessarily come from the same community I did. My family perceived my questions and independent thinking as rebellion. My maternal grandfather, a hypochondriac by nature, admitted to me on his deathbed many years later that throughout my adolescence, he had worried that my way of thinking would someday shock him to death. Despite the forces around me, however, I always stayed true to my own values and morals. My principles became the guiding force in making me who I am today.

Nalini, age 5

Nalini, age 8, with her pet baby goat in Porbandar, a state of Gujarat

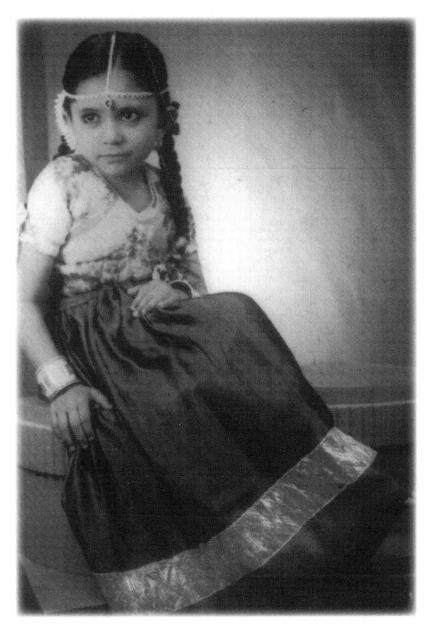

Nalini, age 10, in her Indian dance outfit

Nalini's mother, Sushila, and father, Kantilal

Nalini age 14

Nalini, age 16

7

A Faraway Friend

G.1. Nalini's pen pal, Barbara Steiner

I n my life, I have been fortunate to have many unusual, but truly meaningful, friendships. One of those friendships was with a girl whom I had never met.

When I was fourteen, my high school English teacher told my class about an international agency that encouraged students from all over the world to become pen pals. I was excited about this opportunity to make friends abroad. I had seen pictures of Switzerland with its snow-covered mountains and was fascinated by its beauty. So I requested a pen pal from Switzerland. The agency paired me with a girl from Switzerland who had requested a pen pal from India. We were given each other's addresses.

Barbara wrote the first letter. I was excited to receive a letter from my pen pal. I had never seen even a postage stamp from Switzerland. I saved it for my stamp collection.

Barbara told me that she was fourteen years old and lived in Zurich with her parents and a sister. Her father was in business with people from many different countries. He had worked with people from India, and his stories about them had made her want to have an Indian pen pal. She enclosed a picture of herself. I proudly showed all of my family and friends this picture of my beautiful Caucasian pen pal with blonde hair.

I responded to her letter and sent her a picture of myself. I told her that I hoped to visit Switzerland someday. From then on, Barbara and I wrote letters to each other once a month. We shared stories about our families and schools.

As we grew older, we shared our dreams about what we wanted to do in life. I told Barbara that I wanted to be a doctor and she said that she wanted to be a nurse. In one of her letters, she said that her father had contacts in India, so he could make arrangements for me to go to Switzerland. We fantasized about practicing in the same hospital in Switzerland, me as a doctor and she as a nurse.

Barbara and I continued to write to each other, learning a lot about each other's culture and forming a strong friendship. Eventually, in 1969, just as we had dreamed as teenagers, I graduated from medical school in India and Barbara graduated from nursing school in Switzerland.

Soon Barbara announced that she was going to marry Werner, her high school sweetheart, whom she had told me all about. Werner was an engineer whose assignments took him to different parts of Switzerland, and Barbara would accompany him. But after her marriage, Barbara did not write with her new address. I no longer had a place to send my letters.

Soon after Barbara's marriage, Viren and I got married, and we left for the United States less than a month later. As I planned for my new life in America, I packed many little treasures to bring with me. Among them was the address of Barbara's parents and her photos. A year passed as Viren and I adjusted to our new country. I was too preoccupied with my new life to think about old times and my friendship with Barbara.

However, by that time, Viren and I had saved up some money to travel. Being able to travel had been one of our dreams for our life in the United States. We planned to go to Europe for two weeks with a tour group whose itinerary included two days in Zurich, Switzerland.

I thought about Barbara and our dream that someday we would meet. But I had lost contact with her for almost two years. I felt sad that I had no way to find her when I was in Zurich. Then I remembered that her parents lived in Zurich, and I had brought their address with me when I came to America. I searched through my little treasures from India and, sure enough, I found it.

I wrote to Barbara's mother and asked her to send my letter to Barbara, wherever she was. In that letter, I told her about all the events that had led up to my living in the United States. I also told her that Viren and I would be coming to Europe and shared our itinerary for our stay in Zurich. There was nothing else that I could do.

We arrived in Zurich as planned and checked into our hotel. There was a beautiful lake across from the hotel, and Viren and I decided to go and admire the natural beauty that had first fascinated me about Switzerland.

I sat and watched people walking along the edge of the lake. I wondered, *would a miracle occur to enable me to meet Barbara?* Then again, I thought, *how would I even recognize her?* Though I had seen several photos of her from when we were younger, everyone walking around the lake was Caucasian and looked rather similar to my Indian eyes.

Then I saw a woman with a big smile on her face walking straight toward us. She opened her arms as she approached and said, "You must be Nayna" (my nickname). We embraced tightly, as though we had known each other in person for years. She said that she had spotted me right away because we were the only brown-skinned Indians along the lake.

Barbara told me that she had made a reservation in the hotel where we were staying and had found a room right next to us. We spent two days together, catching up and exchanging stories from the two years that we had been out of touch. Barbara's husband, Werner, was traveling, so we could not meet him, but Viren and Barbara became friends in no time.

As young girls who lived across the oceans and had gotten to know each other solely through letters, Barbara and I had always dreamed that we would meet one day. So seeing her really was a dream come true, after so many years of our meaningful but long-distance friendship.

After Viren and I got home, Barbara and I resumed writing to each other. We promised never to lose contact again. And we didn't. We continued to correspond about the changes and developments in our lives. Two years after we met in Zurich, we shared good news about having our first daughters, Manisha and Monica. Then Barbara had a second daughter, Catherine, and I had my second daughter, Kapila. Subsequently, I had a son, Viral, and Barbara had another daughter, Regula. We talked about the many parallels in our personal lives, which began when we were children and continued through adulthood.

As our families grew, we talked about our travels, our children's dreams, and their marriages. Each year, we sent each other a holiday card, accompanied by a long letter with a summary of our year. Through these holiday cards, we were able to keep in touch despite our busy careers and family lives.

In the summer of 2010, Barbara wrote to me to tell me that she and Werner were planning to visit the United States and would be in New York City for a few days. Viren and I were excited to see them, and I sent her guidebooks, maps, and other materials they could use to plan their visit.

We met in New York, and we also invited Barbara and Werner to visit our home for an Indian dinner (non-spicy). Viren and I were happy to finally meet Werner, and the four of us got along as though we had been friends for years. Barbara and Werner's visit was the highlight of our relationship, which had remarkably started as a pen friendship.

These days, Barbara and I are grandmothers. We talk about our grandchildren and our desire to age gracefully. We share stories about our spiritual lives and the social service work we do through our houses of worship.

Over fifty years ago, Barbara and I became friends without ever having met. Now, after a half century of letters (and now e-mails) and a few brief but memorable visits, our long-distance friendship continues to be strong.

8

I Always Thought I Would See Her Again

Nalini's maternal grandmother, Manima, and maternal grandfather, Nagindas Bakhai ("Bapaji")

A fter I moved to America, I always thought I would see my grandmother, Ma, again. Thankfully, I did. Now that she is gone, I continue to hear her voice in everything I do.

Throughout my young life, Ma was my biggest supporter. She was my greatest source of comfort and wisdom. She always encouraged me to pursue my ambitions. I was the first woman in my community to become a physician. However, my ambition and perseverance to achieve and become somebody came at a big price. In particular, the men in my extended family did not approve of my ambitious thinking. They advised my grandparents to curtail my ambitions because they felt that if I continued to pursue my dreams, my grandparents would never be able to find an appropriate husband for me. Ours was basically a business community in which young men took over their fathers' businesses. Only a very few men in our community pursued higher education and would therefore be acceptable husbands for me if I became a doctor.

From a young age, I despised men who did not think independently and did not pursue their interests. I felt that they were taking the easy way out by joining their family businesses, which had been passed on through several generations. On this issue, as on so many others, I was quite vocal about how I felt. People in my family considered the freedom with which I spoke to be rude and arrogant.

However, my grandmother was different. She listened to what I was saying, helped me clarify my thoughts, and put me on the right track without being judgmental. When I was in medical school, Ma would stay up with me while I was studying late at night. She would make me tea and bring in some snacks so that I could continue to study. My grandmother had never gone to school. She grew up in a small village and learned how to do what I called "women's chores." She came to Mumbai, a large city, after marrying my grandfather at the age of fourteen. In spite of this, she supported my desire to become a doctor.

My ambition to pursue a medical specialty brought me to America in 1970. By then, I had found my life partner, Viren. Our families had arranged our marriage, but we both had had the choice to accept or reject the arrangement. My husband also came from a business community, but, like me, he had the ambition to step out of the familiar life path and had also pursued medicine. Like me, he had planned to pursue a medical specialty in America. We had similar values and similar goals in life. I was twenty-four and Viren was twenty-nine years old.

The first month of our marriage was full of excitement: after our honeymoon, we were going to America, nearly 10,000 miles away from home. No one from our families had ever traveled abroad. As I planned and prepared for the momentous trip ahead, the days passed rapidly.

During that time, I wished I had dedicated some time to sit with my grandmother and ask for her advice on my new marriage and tips for living away from home without any emotional support. Though I had always considered myself an independent thinker, I was scared. It occurred to me that Ma had hardly traveled within India; *how would she know what it would be like to live so far from home?* I brushed those thoughts aside. Deep down, I knew Ma's inspiration would be with me wherever I was.

Finally, our journey to America began, one month after our wedding. Though I was traveling almost 10,000 miles away on a very limited budget, with no set plans to return, I knew that I would see my grandmother again.

In the United States, we discovered that telephone calls to India were very expensive. I spoke to my family once a year and the first thing we said was "We are all right, how is everyone at home?" The phone connections were not very good, and we had to repeat everything several times to be understood, but those phone calls were still something we looked forward to, just to hear each other's voices. However, we mostly communicated through letters.

Ma could not read or write. My mother read my letters to her and wrote to me what Ma wanted me to know. I always wondered where Ma had gained her wisdom about how to live life when she had not received any formal education. She used to repeat her favorite statement, which I have remembered for now over sixty years: "Remember, life is like a knotted ball of wool. Our task is to unknot it strand by strand until each strand flows smoothly again." This statement was deeply meaningful to me. To this day, I think about her words of wisdom when life seems too complicated. I work on unknotting each strand of my life until each one starts flowing smoothly again.

By 1975, we had lived in America for five years. During that time, we had not been back to visit India. One sad morning, a letter arrived from my mother. She said that Ma had been diagnosed with esophageal cancer. She was not able to swallow any solid food. She was weak and mostly staying in bed. My mother said that the doctors did not believe that Ma would live very long.

My husband held my hand as I sat crying and wondering if I would ever see Ma again. I was in the middle of my psychiatry residency. We had saved money for two airline tickets, to be used if we needed to go back home. Our first daughter, Manisha, was one-and-a-half years old at the time. My husband and I both decided to take a week off work to return to India to see my grandmother. We did not inform anyone in India that we were coming. The three of us flew back home to see Ma one last time.

The night before we arrived in India, my grandmother told my grandfather that I had returned to India from the United States. My grandfather called the doctor, who thought she might have been hallucinating and headed for delirium.

We arrived at the Mumbai airport, took a taxi, and arrived at home. When my mother opened the door, we all burst into hysterical laughter from the sheer joy of seeing each other again after so long. My grandmother had a big smile on her face. She said to my grandfather, "Did I not tell you last night that she has come back from the United States?"

My grandfather then told us that when I had left for America in 1970, Ma told him that she wanted to be alive until I was able to return home to see her. As I entered my family's apartment, Ma shouted out loud, "Now, God, you can take me whenever you want, all my desires of life have been fulfilled."

We spent a beautiful week together. Ma told me that she had received in life more than she had asked for. She was able to meet her first great-granddaughter, my firstborn, Manisha.

I knew this was the last time I would see my grandmother. But I was determined to make the most of the week. I instructed family members that none of us should shed tears and those who could not hold back tears had to go to another room until they could compose themselves. My family was surprised to see how emotionally strong I had become. When my grandmother and I were alone, I told her, "You will always be with me: I will always remember your words of wisdom, your unconditional love, your tolerance for my nontraditional thoughts, and your role in making me who I have become."

She said, "I have been always proud of you. I knew the day would come when I would see you return back from the U.S. as a successful physician."

Soon the day of our departure was upon us. We had to say goodbye. Although by then Ma did not walk around the house much because she was so weak, she got up and walked with me to the elevator. We held hands, but did not cry, did not say a word. The elevator door opened, I stepped in, and Ma said, "I will watch over you, I know you will always do the right thing." I nodded my head, still holding onto my tears. We both smiled. As the elevator door closed, tears came rolling down my cheeks. I knew then that my grandmother would not be there the next time I came to India, but I knew that she would always be with me as my guiding torch.

9

My Mother

As the oldest of three siblings, with a sister, Kumud, and a brother, Kantilal, my mother was my grandmother's right hand and my grandfather's wise counsel. She was a brilliant student at Young Ladies High School in Bombay, the school in which she enrolled me as well.

My parents were married young, at nineteen and twenty. My mother stated many times that she and my father had a loving marriage. When they were apart for even a few days, they would write letters to each other. My mother allowed me to read those letters when I was in my teens. Six years after their marriage, when life was beginning to bloom for my parents, a most horrific event occurred: my mother lost her husband, my father, to an acute, sudden, and unexpected abdominal hemorrhage. Her life was over. She expressed it as "Nothing but darkness covered her life." But then she realized that she had a daughter to raise, and an unborn child was growing in her womb.

No one except my father had known about her pregnancy. On the day of my father's funeral, she had enough of a presence of mind to tell a wise aunt that she was pregnant. In those days she would have been called a "whore" if a baby was born after the death of her husband and people did not know she had already been pregnant when he died. At the funeral, the word spread about her pregnancy. Relatives prayed that she be given a baby boy who would grow up and take care of his mother.

My mother was then just twenty-five years old. A second marriage was out of consideration for a widow, who was considered a poor soul, suffering because of her bad *karma*. In several Indian religions, *karma* describes our actions, for which people reap the rewards or suffer the consequences in future incarnations. My mother bought into that belief system and took the role of a victim throughout my growing-up years. She cried easily, blaming her misfortunes on the death of my father.

My mother and I have many similar characteristics. We are both highly organized people who think ahead. However, we have very different outlooks on life. I tend to think positively while my mother concentrates on negative aspects of life.

After the death of my father, my mother turned to religious education. She spent a lot of time with religious elders, learning about *Jainism*, a religion that is based on *Ahimsa* or nonviolence. Later, she taught religious scriptures to young girls.

My mother visited me in New York when my first daughter, Manisha, was born. She was able to adjust to life in the United States rather quickly, but four months later, she returned to India to take care of her aging parents. After my grandmother passed away, my mother and my sister lived by themselves. My sister, a certified laboratory technologist, was the breadwinner.

In 1982, I sponsored my mother and my sister to immigrate to the United States. A few years later, my sister got married and moved to Ardsley, just a five minute car ride from our house. My mother spent her time between our two houses, helping to bring up my sister's daughter,

Bhumi, and my three children. All of them enjoyed the warmth and nurturance from their grandmother.

From early in my life, I felt like I needed to be my mother's and sister's protector and provider. I have taken this responsibility very seriously since early childhood. When I was young, I felt like I was *Jhansi Ki Rani* (see picture): a woman warrior from the 1800s, always pictured with a sword, and a leading figure in the resistance against the British. I fought for both of them like a warrior.

Jhansi Ki Raani is included in the manuscript

As long as I live, I hope to be able to care for my mother. I will do everything in my power to allow her to stay within our home and have her needs met. Only if she becomes very disabled and requires hospitalizations frequently would I consider a nursing home.

In 2000, when my sister passed away while on a trip to Europe, my mother was devastated. But once again, her religion helped her cope rather well. Her strength came from her belief that the soul is immortal and it takes different forms; therefore we should not grieve over loss of mortal things.

From 2000 on, my mother has lived with me. She is eighty-seven years old, physically getting weaker, but mentally very alert. She has continued to teach the scriptures of *Jainism* to young women of our community. Although she had only an eighth-grade education in India, the medium of education in her school was English and she speaks English fluently. In the United States she has not worked, except once a year she would work as an election officer.

Although she has gone through two major losses in her life (the deaths of my father and my younger sister), her soul is amazingly resilient and strong. She refuses to be dependent or to use a wheelchair when she has difficulty walking. During the fire in our house in 2012, she was the first one to smell smoke and alert my housekeeper and the electricians. She was able to get out of the house with her valuable belongings (cell phone and pocketbook) because she has that presence of mind. She is not shaken by the day-to-day trials and tribulations of life. Her negative outlook on life has changed somewhat as a result of her religious studies, and her young students call her on daily basis for spiritual counseling.

10

Journey To The Land Of My Ancestors

Nalini's maternal grandfather, Nagindas Bakhai ("Bapaji"), and paternal grandfather, Chotalal Ghevaria ("Dadaji")

Nalini with Jayant Gandhi (Jaymama)

B oth sides of my family originated in *Porbandar*, a coastal town in Gujarat. My parents, grandparents, and I had lived in Porbandar for a time when I was a young child because it was considered safer than Mumbai during the post-independence Hindu-Muslim riots in the 1940s and 1950s. However, I had always hoped to visit my ancestral home as an adult. Although I knew that the city must have gone through numerous changes in the more than five decades since I had last been there, I hoped that the community had remained close. On my 2013 trip to India, this dream came true.

On January 22, 2013, I went to Porbandar with Jyotsna Vora, my relative and friend, whose ancestors had also originated in Porbandar. Since Jyotsna visits Porbandar often, she was a good guide for me.

My visit to Porbandar was very emotionally charged. My mind was flooded with stories that I had heard from my paternal and maternal grandfathers, Chotalal Prahudas Ghevaria and Nagindas Nanji Bakhai. We saw their homes from the outside and reflected on how the community in Porbandar had stayed so close and provided support to each other during World War II and India's independence movement.

I was also able to spend memorable time with my relatives in *Rajkot*, another ancestor's town on my maternal grandmother's side in Gujarat. I used to spend my summer vacations with my grandmother and her relatives in Rajkot every year from 1962 until 1968. I had not seen these relatives in forty-five years and had never exchanged phone calls, letters, or emails. My cousins had grown-up children and grandchildren whom I had never met, though we had heard about each other through other relatives in Bombay. However, when we met, I connected with them immediately. I was very touched to discover that loving human relationships need no other external connections.

We talked for hours, reminiscing over our past: the time we spent together and the time away from each other, continents apart. My relatives were fascinated to hear my stories, and I was fascinated to hear theirs. They lived modest lives, but their hearts were generous. We expected nothing from each other. I was so grateful to have the opportunity to spend time with them.

While in Porbandar, Jyotsna and I visited a *vandi* (community center). Our ancestors had built the *Porbandar Dasha Shreemali Vanik Samaj Vandi* to be used for community events. It was a large, well-maintained place. We met its caretaker, an elderly gentleman called Hemantbhai and his wife, Nalini. He gave us a tour of the vandi, which is rented out for weddings. They use the money they receive through donations and rental income for the maintenance of the vandi and for the education and medical expenses of the women and children of our samaj (community). Hemantbhai expressed some concern about the future of our samaj's vandi. He said that a number of people from our samaj had moved to Mumbai or abroad and he wished that they would visit Porbandar more often.

We ended our tour of the vandi in the business office. Hemantbhai showed us a large book in which every person who originated in Porbandar was registered. I also saw a large framed photo of Devidas Ghevaria. I was overjoyed that my ancestor had contributed enough to this place to be remembered. My grandfather once told me that our last name, Ghevaria, had been given to us after one of our ancestors had fed the whole town a fancy sweet called *ghevar*.

My uncle, Jayant Gandhi, who was born and raised in Porbandar and who lived in New York City for over thirty years, used to donate money to the vandi every year. Jaymama (as I addressed him in New York) and I did not see each other often, but we talked on the phone. Every year, Jaymama used to tell me how gratified he was to be able to contribute toward the education of the women and children of our samaj. I was very pleased and touched to hear that, after Jaymama passed away, his friend had picked up his annual donation toward our community's welfare. During my visit, following in Jaymama's footsteps, I initiated a similar contribution toward the education and medical expenses of the women and children of our samaj. I felt good that I was continuing my family's tradition of giving back to our community in Porbandar.

While we were there, Jyotsna and I also visited a number of cultural sites, each of which reminded me of the richness of my cultural heritage. One of those sites was *Kirti Mandir*, the memorial temple and museum that has been built around Mahatma Gandhi's (Gandhiji's) ancestral home. Gandhiji was born and brought up in Porbandar, and the room where he lived is well preserved . . . During my visit to Kirti Mandir, I was delighted to learn that many of the historical pictures that were in the museum will be soon digitalized for protection. I was born on January 26, 1946, which is the date when India became a republic. The independence movement in India was initiated by one man who wore one piece of cloth; that was Mahatma Gandhi. It was exhilarating to stand on the earth where his house stood.

We also visited the *Krishna-Sudama Mandir*, a temple dedicated to Sudama. Sudama was the poor but generous friend of Krishna. In the story, Sudama and Krishna met at a *gurukul* (a school away from home under the supervision of a guru and his wife, a guruma). I was fascinated to learn that Porbandar had previously been called *Sudamapuri*, because of the importance of Sudama in Porbandar's history.

Another wonderful place we visited was the *Bharat Museum*, which has an amazing collection of statues of religious, historical, and political figures who have contributed to the greatness of *Bharat* (India). Under each statue was an inspiring quote. We spent several hours in this museum, reading and pondering over these words. I was also touched by the contribution made by Nanji Kalidas, a philanthropic gentleman who has migrated to Africa and who donated the resources to build the Bharat Museum and a number of other such places in Porbandar.

On our last day in Porbandar, we visited a small factory where *khajala* (a savory snack) are made. Porbandar is well known for making khajala with pure *ghee* (butter). I remember my grandparents talking about the health benefits of Porbandar's pure ghee. We were given a tour of the factory and an opportunity to roll and fry a couple of khajala ourselves.

As we were watching the khajala being made, a family that lived next door to the factory came out to meet us and offer us tea and snacks. Sitting with them on their front porch, we learned how three generations of their family lived together in a very simple but loving life. They opened their hearts by telling us that their provider son was driving a taxi and their two young grandchildren were in school. They planned to educate their granddaughter as well as their grandson, perhaps with the hope that someday they will go to the United States for higher education. They were curious about our visit to Porbandar and our interest in coming to this small factory and even trying to learn how to make khajala; they knew that most tourists would find khajala in the big stores in the cities. I was touched by their openness and lack of formality, and we took some pictures to remember our time with them.

Both evenings that I was in Porbandar, I walked along the beautiful and well-maintained shoreline. While watching the sun set and thinking about my trip, I felt fulfilled. This journey to the land of my ancestors offered me an opportunity to examine how richer this trip had made me.

My visit reminded me that, though I had not lived in Porbandar since I was a child, the community there was my community. I was delighted also to have visited Rajkot and have met a new generation of relatives, with whom I had bonded instantly. I was happy to be able to continue my family's legacy of contributing to the strength and betterment of the Porbandar community. Finally, my trip reminded me of the important contributions of the people of Porbandar and renewed my pride in my cultural heritage.

I bade goodbye to Porbandar and to Rajkot with tears in my eyes. I was not sure if I would ever return, but I left with wonderful memories to take back with me and share with my family in the United States.

11

The Next Generations

Nalini and Viren's family: Manisha, Viren in rear row,
Nalini, Viral, and Kapila

Our first child, a beautiful baby girl, Manisha, was born on January 21, 1973. I was able to spend the first two years of her life at home with her. When she was two years old, I started my psychiatry residency. The wife of one of the doctors in our hospital took care of Manisha while I was at work. She had two teenage children. She was loving and kind, almost like a grandmother to Manisha, and I trusted her judgment. She was Korean, and she told me later that she had learned English with Manisha while they watched "Sesame Street" together on television.

We lived in one of the three tall towers that offered housing for medical students, residents, and faculty at the Albert Einstein College of Medicine in the Bronx. During the summer months, when I arrived home from work in the evening, I would find Manisha playing in the sandbox with other children from the building. One day, the security guard, who usually stood outside where the children played, asked me if Manisha was my daughter. I said yes, but I wondered why he asked. He told me he was amazed to see how my five-year-old daughter took charge and organized the play with other children. He said, "Mark my words; she will be a future leader."

I have often reflected on this security guard's words. At five years old, Manisha displayed an ability to lead others that she has built upon in each stage of her life. Manisha is a clear thinker and is well organized. I have been so proud to watch and support her as she built a stellar career as an infectious disease specialist, Associate Professor of Medicine at Yale Medical School, and Director of the Infectious Disease Fellowship program at Yale University Hospital. She attended Ivy League universities for each stage of her education: the University of Pennsylvania for college, Cornell University for medical school and residency training, and Yale University for fellowship training. She is married to Raj, her undergraduate sweetheart. They have given us two beautiful grandchildren, a daughter, Ishani, and a son, Shaan.

After I completed my psychiatry residency, on June 8, 1978, Viren and I welcomed our second daughter, Kapila (we call her Kapi). Kapi wanted to do everything that her older sister did. When she was three years old, she learned to do math in her head. Watching her then, we knew that she would excel at anything she wanted to do.

When Kapi was six years old, Viren encouraged her to enter a Mother's Day drawing contest, which required children ages five to ten to submit drawings that described their mothers. Kapi drew a picture of me and identified me as "Supermom." In her drawing, I stood in a white coat and stethoscope, next to a car in the center of the drawing. On the periphery around me were the school, playground, a grocery store, our kitchen, and the hospital. My perceptive little girl had depicted her mother carrying out all of these different roles. She won first prize, and it was the best Mother's Day gift of my life. I was proud that my daughter saw me as a Supermom; she made me realize that I had fulfilled the wishes of my grandfather who had wanted me to be both a professional person and a mother at the same time.

Kapi is multi-talented and grew to be a creative and expressive girl. In high school, she played a number of roles in school musicals. During her senior year, she played the lead role in the musical "South Pacific." She continued to sing, in *a capella* group, throughout her college years at Yale University.

Kapi then went to law school at New York University, where she met her husband, Hrishi. She worked at a law firm, Sullivan & Cromwell LLC, and the Transportation

Security Administration, and stayed home for a short time to raise her young kids and make homemade meals every day. Kapi and Hrishi have raised two beautiful and smart children, a boy, Kush, and a girl, Piya.

Though Viren and I had a complete family of four, we really wanted a son. Our friends shared their experience with us as a warning: they had two daughters, planned a third pregnancy hoping for a boy, and ended up with twin girls. Despite this warning, we decided to try to have a son.

When I was pregnant for the third time, I had a sonogram that showed the shadow of the baby's genitalia: it was a boy! We were overjoyed! However, we did not share this news with anyone. Manisha was eight and Kapila was three years old at the time. In Indian culture, male children are given excessive importance. But we wanted to make sure that our girls did not feel less important.

On June 2, 1981, our son, Viral, was born. Viral grew up to be a charmer. He had (and has) a smile that won everyone over and made it very difficult for me to discipline him. He was admired by his teachers and friends alike. In fact, his preschool teacher made a tie-dyed t-shirt for him when he moved on to kindergarten. The shirt read, "You are the sunshine of my life."

In high school, Viral played soccer, sang, and played the drums. He went to college at the University of Pennsylvania, where he sang for the world's first Hindi *a capella* singing group named "Penn Masala." He went on to medical school at Yale University. While there, he told me that he wanted to be an ophthalmologist to help people with diminished vision regain their eyesight and someday travel internationally to participate in medical camps.

Viral's dream has come true. He did his ophthalmology residency at New York Eye and Ear Hospital (New

York University), and completed cornea fellowships at Philadelphia's Wills Eye Institute and the Cleveland Clinic. He is admired by his mentors and well respected by his patients. He is married to his neurosurgeon wife, Rupa.

In 1980 we build a house on a lake in the Poconos. Every weekend while the children were in elementary and middle school, we went to the Poconos and went sailing in our boat. While our children were young, our family of five also traveled together extensively, both within the United States, including Alaska, and internationally, throughout Europe and Asia. Viren documented our travels with his video camera and I always took pictures.

These travels provided me and Viren with a wonderful opportunity to bond with each other and with our children. In the relaxed environment of our vacations, away from school and work, we were able to learn about each of our children's special talents and the intricacies of their personalities. These were some of my most memorable times.

I learned that Manisha could look up directions with Viren and guide everyone to our destination. She was also the consummate big sister, always watching over her younger siblings. During our trips, we often split up into a "boys' team" and a "girls' team." My two girls and I loved to shop in every port of our travels, and the boys' team watched television after a long day of tourist activities . . .

Every time we returned home, Viral renamed the bathrooms in our house as "Men's Room" and "Women's Room." He wanted to use our master bathroom with his dad because he decided that it was the "Men's Room" where his team could comb their hair and talk as they did on vacation. We were all amused by his sense of humor, but we had to remind him that our trip was over and we were back to the usual routine in our house.

Together, we faced the challenges of traveling as well. For example, we told our kids about our experiences as immigrants in our early days in America. The Indian government had allowed us to come to America with only $8.00. We had borrowed from Viren's brother to pay for the airline tickets. We also told them that our first vacation was to Canada. We drove from Highland Park, Michigan, to Niagara Falls, Toronto, Montreal, and Quebec on a very small budget. In spite of that, we had saved $1000 in one year; of this, $400 were used up on the trip. We stayed in motels each night. These motels cost us $8 per night. In those days vegetarian food was not easily available. We would eat salad, bread, and French fries for lunch and pizza for dinner every day. Once we had driven from New York to Florida over two days and stayed at roadside motels. At one motel we could not shower because the water had high levels of sulfuric acid and it smelled awful. Ever since then, whenever we stayed at a roadside motel we would ask to see the room first and check the running water in the bathroom before signing up to stay.

The more they knew about the challenges we had faced, the more resilient they became, and they could moderate the effects of stress. We worked hard to teach them that they belonged to something bigger than themselves.

One of the accomplishments that I am most proud of is that all three of our children were recognized as "Miss Edgemont" or "Mr. Edgemont" by Edgemont High School. This honor was given to those graduates who had not only excelled academically but had also showed integrity of character and made Edgemont High School proud.

As I entered the sixth decade of my life, I thought I had already fulfilled my dreams of having a career and raising a family. I did not realize that the best phase of my life was yet to begin.

On November 12, 2000, our first granddaughter, Ishani, daughter of Manisha and Raj, was born. Becoming a *Nani* (Gujarati for grandmother—specifically, mother's mother) has been a thrill that I could not have imagined. As grandparents, we have had the pleasure of nurturing our grandchildren, reading them stories, taking them to events, and sharing values, without needing to be their disciplinarians. We have always told our grandchildren that we have to follow their parents' rules and have tried not to give them mixed messages or spoil them.

Ishani was a smart and take-charge little girl, just like her mother. When she was about three years old, I taught her to eat by herself by bringing her mouth close to her plate rather than bringing the food to her mouth. I did not know that such a young child could process information and remember it so well, so I was shocked when one day Viren dropped food on his shirt and Ishani told him, "*Nana* (grandpa), bring your mouth close to your plate." We all had to laugh.

I always loved buying Ishani Indian outfits when I visited India. Each time she outgrew one, Ishani would say, "Nani, it is time for you to visit India." I love to watch her perform Indian folk dances, which Manisha choreographs for her. Just as Manisha, Kapi, and Viral did as children, Ishani performs Indian folk dances with her friends, learning about and sharing her culture. When I had choreographed dances for all three of our children, I felt that I had contributed towards introducing Indian culture. I am so proud that they have now passed it on to their children.

Raj and Manisha's son, Shaan, was born on December 5, 2003. Ishani was with us the night before Raj and Manisha were to go to the hospital for a planned cesarean section. When we went there to meet baby Shaan, we dressed Ishani in a t-shirt that read "Big Sister." Shaan was the cuddliest little boy and was content most of the time. Just like Viral, Shaan used his sweet smile to get away with a lot of mischief!

As Shaan has gotten older, he has displayed some unique talents. He used to say that he liked to collect things people throw away. To Manisha's annoyance, Shaan could not throw anything out. He has a creative mind and loves to build, so he uses what he finds and creates something new out of it. He has been an active Indian folk dancer as well. Ishani and Shaan make the cutest Indian folk dancers.

On October 24, 2007, Hrishi and Kapila's baby boy, Kush, was born. At that time, Kapila and Hrishi lived in Washington, D.C. We received a call late at night, informing us that Kapi's water had broken and she was going to the hospital. First thing the next morning, Viren and I started on our trip to meet our new grandson. I still remember the surge of love I felt when we held him for the first time and I saw his smile.

I stayed with Kapi and her family for two weeks after Kush's birth. Halloween was a week after Kush was born, and I wished we could find a first Halloween costume for him. Sure enough, while I was wandering in a Halloween store, I saw a costume that looked like a chilly pepper (Viren's favorite). I bought it and then Kapi and I stuffed it with rags and placed one-week-old baby Kush in the costume. He looked adorable.

I have been fascinated by the way Kush talks and processes information at a very young age. Kush has a very curious mind, and he always wants to learn about how things function, from toilets to machines. Kapi and Hrishi have been equal partners in enhancing Kush's curiosity and enriching his mind.

Kush's favorite word has always been "Why?" We can always respond using difficult words. He will quickly ask if he does not understand a word and immediately learns to use these words appropriately. One time, I told Kush that if we don't get things exactly the way we want, we should not be upset because we have to learn to be flexible. A few days later, a similar episode occurred in his class at school. Kush told his teacher that "We have to be flexible." The teacher was very impressed by this little boy's understanding of words and his ability to use them correctly.

Kush has a tree-nut allergy. I have admired Kapi's dedication in explaining Kush's allergy to him, and cooking and baking for him for every occasion, so that he never has to feel deprived because he cannot have some treat that everyone else can have.

On February, 5, 2010, Kapi gave birth to her daughter, Piya. She was born one day before Viren's birthday and from the beginning was Nana's girl. Piya has beautiful curly long hair. She is in love with her big brother, Kush, and is his "baby bear." Kush is Piya's 'protector bear". She repeats everything that Kush says verbatim.

One day, I wondered if Piya actually thinks on her own. I whispered to Kush that he should say, "Piya is a bad girl." Immediately, Piya replied, "Kush is a bad boy." I laughed hysterically—*clearly she did think independently.*

Our grandchildren have given us plenty to muse on. As a grandparent, I regret that I did not write down all the memorable stories at the time they happened. Our grandchildren have made us laugh, cry, and gaze with wonder. They make my day. However, I am most fulfilled to see that our children have continued to pass on the morals and cultural values that we taught them to the next generation.

I had great pleasure in writing this essay. I am fully aware that, like all parents and grandparents, I feel that my children and grandchildren are the most wonderful ever!

Kidding aside, my Hindu way of thinking reminds me that children, grandchildren were given to us. We don't own them. We may have been instrumental in their successes to some extent, but really, they came to us with their own karma, and became successful through their own efforts as well. When pride overrides my emotions, I try to remember to be grateful that I have such children and grandchildren.

Nalini with Manisha, Kapila, and Viral in their lakefront house in the Poconos

Manisha and Kapila tying rakhee on Viral at Raksha Bandhan, an annual Indian festival (rakhee is a symbolic band that signifies a bond of best wishes between sisters and brothers)

Manisha as a choreographer of an Indian folk dance; Viral was the youngest dancer

Manisha graduates from the University of Pennsylvania

Kapila graduates from New York University Law School

Manisha and Raj's daughter Ishani

Manisha and Raj's son, Shaan, in his dance outfit

Kapila and Hrishi's son, Kush

Nalini with Kapila and Hrishi's son Kush

Nalini and Viren's four grandchildren: Piya, Ishani, Kush and Shaan

Part III

Values Through Adversity

12

Enduring Values

As an adult, I am often transported back to moments of my childhood, which I remember as vividly as though they had happened yesterday. Whenever I fail to live up to the values with which I was raised, I am reminded of the lessons of my childhood.

Several years after we had moved to America, Viren and I were driving home one day. He made a left turn, and in moments we heard a police siren. The police officer told us to pull the car over. I was terrified, and my husband was numb. We had no idea why we had been stopped. As we sat there, Viren wondered if it was because we had made a left turn where there was a sign that said "No Left Turn from 7:30 am to 4:30 pm." I looked at my watch: it was 4:25 pm. The car's clock said 4:25 pm as well. I quickly changed the time on my watch and the car's clock to 4:35pm.

Just then, the officer appeared and checked my husband's driver's license and registration. Sure enough, his guess had been accurate; we had been pulled over because of that left turn. I showed the officer the time on our car's clock and my watch. The officer gave me a piercing look, looked at his own watch, made a phone call, and finally said, "You have the wrong time."

I told the officer that we were doctors and had set our watches based on the hospital clock. His attitude softened

101

when he heard the word "doctors." He gave us a warning, asked us to keep the correct time, and let us leave without any penalty. What a sigh of relief!

My husband and I were silent for a while. I was deep in thought. Though we had not gotten a traffic ticket, I did not feel good about what had happened. I had been dishonest and had not been true to my values. As I reflected on what I had done, I was reminded of a lesson from my childhood.

When I was in kindergarten, my cousin and I went to school together, and we were great playmates. He was six months older than me. We enjoyed playing with a toy train in the classroom. One day, my cousin suggested that we take this train home so that we could play with it there. So we did.

That afternoon, my mother was surprised that we were so quiet, and she saw that we were playing with a toy she had not seen before. She asked us about this train, and I volunteered that we had taken it from school. She asked us if our teacher had given us permission to bring this train home. I replied that we had not asked for her permission.

My mother was visibly upset. She immediately took us back to school, told us to apologize to the teacher for "stealing" the toy, and had us return it to her. I learned for the first time what stealing meant. I have a vivid memory of feeling ashamed when I apologized to the teacher. My cousin was quiet and he did not say anything. The teacher was thankful to my mother for teaching us a valuable lesson. I remember that day every time I share my childhood stories with my children and grandchildren. Though my cousin and I had not intended to be dishonest, our action did equate to stealing. Children have to be taught the meaning of their actions, which may have come from ignorance. I was fortunate that the value of being truthful was instilled in me as a child.

My older daughter, Manisha, who has two children, once went on a family vacation to the Cayman Islands. Their hotel was a ferry ride away from some stores they had visited. While on the ferry headed back to their hotel, Manisha's husband noticed that their six-year-old daughter, Ishani, had two similar toys in her hands, though they had bought only one.

Manisha asked her about the second toy, and Ishani said that she had picked it up for her little brother. Both parents were upset, and to teach Ishani the right values, they took another ferry back to the store and had Ishani return the toy for which they had not paid. The storekeeper told Ishani to keep the toy as a gift from her and praised her parents for taking the time while on vacation to teach their child that taking things without paying for them is called stealing and it is dishonest to do so.

On their return from their vacation, Manisha told me this story and said that she was thinking about the story from my childhood, which I had told her when she was a child. I was so happy to learn that three generations had now processed and passed on the valuable lesson that my mother had taught me.

13

Nurturing and Teaching

Nalini in her role as Residency Training Director with Dolores King,
the residency coordinator

I have always received the most gratification and fulfillment from the process of nurturing and teaching. I was fortunate to spend twenty-five years of my career as residency training director for psychiatry at Bronx Lebanon Hospital. In that position, I was able to nurture, teach, evaluate, and provide feedback to more than 120 psychiatry residents as well as more than 450 medical students, preparing them to practice not only the science of medicine but also the art of curing, caring, and healing the sufferer. My career as an educator gave me the opportunity to shape the professional lives of my trainees in significant ways.

I completed my specialty training in psychiatry on June 30, 1978. I had just given birth to my second daughter, Kapila, and planned to work as a psychiatrist part-time and spend the rest of my time enjoying being a mother of two daughters. However, my chairman of psychiatry at Bronx Lebanon Hospital had a different plan for me.

The chairman offered me the position of residency training director just four months after I completed my own residency. He assured me that he had faith that I was the right candidate for the position. Viren and I discussed the offer, and Viren encouraged me to accept it because he knew that I hoped to be an educator one day. He also suggested that we could hire a full-time live-in housekeeper to take care of the children and do housework while we were both at work.

In 1979, I began my new job. I was the first psychiatry residency training director in the country who was a woman, of color, and a graduate of a medical school outside the United States. I called myself a "triple minority." It was an intimidating thought.

Our training program was located in an inner-city hospital, and many American-trained doctors were not interested in pursuing their specialty training in such a hospital. However, we attracted the best and the brightest graduates from international medical schools, who did not have the opportunity to train in the large academic centers that American-trained doctors favored. Our trainees came to us from all over the world: Russia, China, Korea, the Philippines, India, Pakistan, Bangladesh, Nigeria, Ghana, Puerto Rico, Colombia, Venezuela, Ecuador, Haiti, and the Dominican Republic, to name a few. I fondly called our training program the "United Nations."

I learned very quickly that to train graduates from these and other countries, I had to be astutely aware of their cultures, since their cultures determined their behavior and their way of thinking. They had to learn not only the culture of our American patients, who were predominantly African-American or Hispanic, but also how to get along with colleagues and peers from a variety of backgrounds.

During my twenty-five years as residency training director, my residency coordinator was a caring woman named Dolores. Dolores and I were both on the same mission. We wanted to nurture and teach residents. Dolores was my confidante and advisor on many occasions.

My job as residency training director became my career. I was one of the very few training directors in the country to stay in the position for twenty-five years. Most of my interactions with my residents were highly rewarding, but I cannot forget three of my most difficult experiences. They challenged me by testing the boundaries and limitations of what I could and could not do for my residents as their training director. One of my most challenging experiences occurred during my first year as a training director.

Dr. J

Dr. J was in the first month of her psychiatry residency, and I was already being bombarded with phone calls and negative evaluations: "Where did you find her?" "She does not understand directions given to her." "She cannot carry out orders." "Get her out of my unit."

Dr. J was from Bangladesh, and she barely understood the system in which she was working. She looked different to those supervisors who watched her take care of patients. She was terrified of her supervisors and was constantly anxious.

I wondered how I could help her. I had to tell her that her supervisors were completely disappointed with her performance. I called her into my office and presented the problem to her. She listened very intently. But she did not seem affected by this negative feedback.

Why? I wondered why she watched my lip movements so intently. I wondered if she really heard me. A thought occurred to me: *could she be having difficulty hearing?* But if that were so, how could she have come so far without a hearing aid?

During the week after my meeting with Dr. J, I received additional harsh criticism from her supervisors every day. The chairman of the psychiatry department summoned me to his office. He said he had heard that a new resident was in deep trouble and asked me to make a decision about her, implying that I needed to fire her.

I was inexperienced in my new job. Timidly, I mentioned that I had met with Dr. J and suspected that she might have hearing problems. To address my suspicion, I wanted to send her for an evaluation by an ear, nose, and throat (ENT) specialist. Her supervisors, who were experienced teachers and also my colleagues, laughed at my suggestion.

My chairman was clearly irritated. He said, "As a training director, you will have to make tough decisions," and told me that I was messing up early in my career.

Despite my chairman's and colleagues' derision, I decided to send Dr. J to an ENT for an evaluation. To everyone's surprise but mine, Dr. J returned with a hearing aid. Every day her performance improved dramatically. Dr. J was grateful that she was given a chance to do a better job, and I was gratified that I had been able to make a meaningful difference in her life. The experience taught me that, as training director, I would often face multiple forces pulling me in different directions, but that I had to trust my own gut feeling and sometimes take a risk.

Dr. P

Dr. P had an unusual family background: he was born to a French mother and an African-American father in the Philippines where his father was stationed as a serviceman. His mother had died of cancer when he was a teenager, and his father never remarried. Dr. P had sailed through medical school and was recruited to be a psychiatric resident in our program.

Dr. P had a good rapport with me, though I noticed that he was rather aloof from his peers. At the end of one uneventful year of residency, he decided to pursue acting for a while, which he said he had wanted to do all his life. He left our program with our blessings.

After his departure, I did not hear from him for several years. Then one day he returned, looking to rejoin our program for his second year of residency. But I did not have a position open for him. He was disappointed but accepted a position in another program in a different state.

On the day that Dr. P signed his contract for his new residency; he left the hospital and on his way home, got out of his car for a moment on a busy street. Inexplicably, he pulled out a gun and fired two shots, killing two insurance agents who were walking down the street on their way to lunch. He made his way to his home, where police found him after receiving some leads. He put up no resistance and has been imprisoned ever since.

Three years after the shooting, around Christmas, Dr. P wrote me a letter. He sent his regards to the residency program's secretary and asked me about his classmates and their whereabouts. He also asked me to get him out of prison. Though I had heard about the shooting through police inquiries and in the newspapers, his unusual request came as a surprise to me. My heart ached when I read his pleas.

I wondered if I should reply to his letter. Instead, I sent him a Christmas card and prayers for peace. After that, he wrote to me every few months, and I began to notice some disconnected thoughts and grandiose ideas in his letters. I collected the letters in his training file but never responded. I wondered where my responsibility as a training director ended and where my human instinct to help him began. Yet I knew that despite my sympathy, I could not do anything for him.

Dr. R

Dr R. was of Indian origin and a first-year psychiatry resident. During his four-month family medicine rotation (a requirement to complete the first year in psychiatry), he made an appointment to come and see me. I asked him about his training in the family medicine program, his family, and his wellbeing. He said that his wife was in India visiting her family for a month. He expressed no concerns about the family medicine training. I knew that he had been doing well at work because I had received good reports from his supervisors during the first two months of his rotation. He thanked me for giving him the time to visit me. As he left, I wondered what was the real reason he had come to see me.

Two days later, I received a frantic call from one of his fellow residents. Dr. R had not reported for work. When his fellow resident went to see him in his on-call room in the hospital, Dr. R did not open the door. A security guard forced the door open, and they saw Dr. R on the floor in a pool of blood. He had killed himself by slitting his throat.

Everyone in our residency program was shocked and also saddened that we had not realized that he needed help. I replayed our conversation from two days earlier in my head, but I did not feel that he had given me any clues. I contacted his wife when she returned to the United States. She too had been shocked by Dr. R's suicide. He had called her the day before he killed himself, but their conversation had been routine and he had displayed no signs of depression or impulsivity that could have led to his tragic suicide. Dr. R had not even given us a chance to intervene, though I now understood that he had come to say goodbye, in his own way.

My heart ached for my residents when they were going through difficult times. I took a long time to come to terms with the limitations on my ability to do what was best for them.

Over the years, I trained residents who were gay and had AIDS. They had never shared these details with their own parents, but they did share them with me. One former resident with AIDS called me from a hospital in Puerto

Rico. I was very fortunate to be able to talk to him and comfort him, because he died shortly thereafter.

I always saw each trainee as more than just a student or worker in the hospital; I tried to understand each as a human being. Because of that, I felt a closer bond with each of them and I think they felt a closer bond with me. When I left Bronx Lebanon after twenty-five years, grown men cried. That told me something about the impact I had had.

14

Lessons From My Taxi Drivers

In my job as a Field Reprentative for the Accreditation Council for Graduate Medical Education (ACGME), I have traveled all over the country, from the biggest cities to the smallest of small towns. Every other week (I work part-time); I have been in a new place, reviewing new residency programs and meeting new people. Through this journey, I have learned so much about our country and the people in it. Some of my greatest lessons have come from taxi drivers, who have been so much more than just my chauffeurs: they have been my tour guides, my companions, my teachers, and when I was lucky, my very good friends.

Some of my taxi drivers have been immigrants from various parts of the world. I have talked to them about their countries of origin, their cultures, their vocations, and their trials and tribulations in the United States. Several of them have been accomplished professionals, some of them educated and very smart. When possible, some of them have driven me on all of the short rides between my hotel and the hospitals where I was working.

Having the same driver for four days in a row, on several short rides, also allowed me to learn about their aspirations. One taxi driver in Charlottesville, Virginia, told me that he was a refugee. With the help of the social services that this country provided to him, he was able to become a tax-paying citizen. By the time I met him, he owned three cars, employed other immigrants, and helped them get on their feet.

I identify with these immigrant taxi drivers' initial struggle for survival and their aspirations to make their American Dream come true. The high point of these short encounters has always been when a taxi driver shakes my hand after my last taxi ride, gives me his personal phone number, and says, "Call me when you come back, I will be waiting to pick you up."

Of all of my taxi drivers, the one I got to know best was Lester, who drove me back and forth from my Scarsdale home to the New York City airports every other week. Over the course of five years, I took more than 200 one-hour rides in his car.

Lester was always punctual when he picked me up and always wanted to know where I was flying. He knew that I would be taking several short taxi rides during each four-day trip. He advised me to get to know my taxi drivers. Since he knew I was a psychiatrist, sometimes he would say, "Doc, give them one of your tests and check them out to make sure they are safe." At the end of each trip, Lester was waiting for me at the airport in New York to drive me home.

In the five years that I knew him, we became good friends. Lester and I truly enjoyed talking to each other. We talked about everything, from culture to politics to social life. Our conversations felt completely natural. We never needed to resort to small talk.

In talking with Lester, I learned a lot about him. He was an electrical engineer who had worked for twenty years on Long Island. After retirement, he started to drive a taxi.

He was married and had one grown-up daughter who was seriously dating a guy that Lester liked.

Lester had profound practical wisdom. For example, he told me he had recommended that his daughter and her boyfriend get their credit checked before they decided to get married, so that they would know about any financial issues ahead of them. He told me that young people think about getting pre-nuptial agreements, or getting their blood tested for AIDS, but they do not think about getting each other's credit checked, even though most young married couples fight over finances. I thought his advice was wise and very thoughtful.

During our rides, I shared with Lester a lot about my background. Lester was very curious about how I had gotten to where I was today. He asked interesting questions about my experiences, both in India as well as when I first came to America. He was particularly intrigued by my history of challenging the norms of both tradition-bound Indian society and the "boys' club" of medical academia in America.

One day, after hearing one of my many stories, Lester said, "Doc, you are an uncompromising activist." I was struck by how insightful his observation was. I thought that he had very accurately described me, because I have always been uncompromising in my advocacy for the positions I believed in. I was also struck by how well Lester knew and understood me, despite the fact that we had gotten to know each other in his taxi cab. Frequently, I ruminated on this title "An uncompromising activist"

I once told Lester that someday I would write a memoir that would include a chapter on the "lessons from my taxi drivers." I said that our conversations would be a large part of this chapter. He asked me to make sure to write that

Lester, my taxi driver, had called me an "uncompromising activist."

Although we had very different backgrounds, Lester and I shared a common value system. Lester was a Republican, and I had, until very recently, also been a registered Republican. However, neither of us had ever voted along party lines.

Our talks were particularly interesting during the presidential campaign of 2008. We really bonded, because of our mutual belief that Barack Obama shared our values and should be the next president. We both changed our party registration prior to the primaries so that we could vote for Barack Obama. Despite his support of Obama, during the Democratic primary campaign between Obama and Hillary Clinton, Lester said he believed that in a presidential election, the American people would elect a white man over a black man and a black man over a woman. He did not expect that he would ever see one of his own, a black man become president in his lifetime.

I was in Baltimore, Maryland, on election night, November 4, 2008. Lester was watching the election results in New York and I was watching them in Baltimore. When CNN announced that Barack Obama would be the next president of the United States, we both danced for joy. Lester called me a few minutes later on my cell phone, something he had never done before. We both were overjoyed, not just because it was a historic moment, and not just because Barack Obama would be the first black president, but because we truly shared our new president's values.

In early 2009, I took my annual one-month vacation in India. When I returned, I saw that Lester had lost a lot of weight. I inquired how my heavy-set friend had lost so much weight in such a short time. He said he didn't know. His weight loss did not bother him, but he hated that he did not look forward to meals the way he used to. Lester had loved to eat; Philly cheese steaks had been his favorite.

I urged Lester to get a medical checkup, which he did. Sadly, he found out that he had pancreatic cancer. I knew that patients with this type of cancer did not normally survive for more than two to three years after the diagnosis was made. With his regular chemotherapy and radiation therapy treatments, Lester could not drive me in his taxi as regularly as he had before, but he never missed calling to tell me how his treatment was progressing. He was optimistic, but I could see that he was getting weaker. Some days, I was the only passenger he drove all day. In spite of this, we never talked about death or dying.

I was at the Chicago airport when I received a call from Lester's daughter. Lester had asked her to tell me that he was stopping all treatments. I told her I would like to visit him at his home the next day, since I would be returning from Chicago. But before I could do this, Lester's daughter called again with the sad news that my taxi driver, my dear friend, Lester, had passed away.

I attended Lester's funeral, at which several of his college friends, his daughter and some family members who had come from out of town spoke. One friend described Lester's loyalty as a friend when he had financial difficulties in college. Another friend said that Lester was an early riser. He would start driving his cab at 4.00 am. By 7.00 am he would call up his friend and say it was bright daylight, he had already worked for three hours, and it was about time for his friend to wake up. This friend called Lester his alarm clock. He said he would miss his early morning chats with Lester.

At the funeral I met Lester's wife and daughter for the first time. They were very pleased to meet me because now they could put my face to the description Lester had given them of me. His wife said with tears in her eyes that Lester had looked forward to driving me in his cab. He told them that I was his favorite doctor friend.

I think often of this beautiful and unique friendship. It was an unusual relationship, but one in which we shared so much with each other.

15

Awareness of Mortality

I knew I needed help.
I have always been a very independent and self-sufficient person. Having lost my father at a very young age, I always had to be able to take care of myself. It took a life-changing moment for me to acknowledge that I needed help.

One day in October, 1985, I woke up at 6:00 am. It was a special day. I had directed and choreographed a dance for a small group that had been invited to perform at the Lincoln Center library. Being a first-generation immigrant from India, I took great pleasure in sharing our culture with mainstream America through Indian dance, music, clothing, and jewelry. I had taught my American-born daughters, Manisha, then ten years old, and Kapila, then five, to perform an Indian folk dance with eight other girls of Indian origin. We had performed in many places, but this was our first appearance at the Lincoln Center library. We were delighted to have this recognition.

I went to the bathroom to get ready for our exciting day. Whoops . . . something strange happened in my head. "Wow, what was that all about?" I wondered. I looked in the mirror and saw nothing—just black. I took a deep breath and opened my eyes again. I saw two of everything and then got dizzy, all within moments.

I went back to my bed and closed my eyes, but my thoughts were racing. My pulse throbbed loudly in my ears. My mind was clear, and my clinician's mind was at work. I rushed through all of the potential diagnoses of what I had just experienced. Could this be a bleeding brain aneurysm or a brain tumor that just burst? In any case, whatever was happening, I concluded that the outcome was going to be dismal. In this situation, I had to be the patient, not the doctor.

I quickly woke Viren. After hearing my detailed description of what I had experienced, he did a quick neurological exam, and then he was silent. He had seen nystagmus (my eyes flickering from right to left) and had heard me describe diplopia (double vision), which explained the dizziness I was experiencing.

I wished I could open my eyes to see his reaction, but I couldn't. With my eyes closed, however, I could tell that he was numb. Finally, he said we had to go to the hospital and find a neurosurgeon.

I knew I needed help, but we were expected to perform at Lincoln Center. Even though my condition could have been deadly, my thinking was crystal clear. I called the mothers of all of the girls and explained what was going on. I told them to take the girls to the Lincoln Center library and let them perform without me.

It was hard for me to explain to my daughters why I had my eyes closed and why they had to leave without me. I blessed them and told them that when they were dancing, I would be watching them through the window in my mind and feeling very proud of them. Reluctantly, with tears in their eyes, they kissed me and left. I held back tears, but even with my eyes closed, salty drops found their way down my cheeks.

This episode was a marker in my life.

I believed that I was very close to dying. When we left the house, I knew I would be hospitalized, but I did not think it was necessary to take a bag of clothes and toiletries. I thought I might not live to see the next day.

After a lot of testing in the hospital, the CT scan showed a small bleed in my mid-brain. The neurosurgeon told us that no surgeon would be willing to try to remove this type of clot. The next twenty-four hours would be critical. Somehow, I was not afraid. I sang to my husband, "Que sera sera, whatever will be will be, the future's not ours to see." I kissed him and gave him a tight hug. Both of us were holding back tears. I sent him home to be with the kids, and I fell asleep.

I woke up the next morning, again thinking clearly. I touched my hand and face and said to myself, *I am alive.* I was afraid to open my eyes. I lay in bed for a few more minutes and then I mustered the courage to open them. Wow! The double vision and dizziness were gone.

The clot in my brain had started to diminish in size, which took the pressure off the vital parts of my brain. When the neurosurgeon arrived, he said that I must have had a small capillary bleed that was not part of a more serious arteriovenous anomaly (an abnormal connection between arteries and veins), which he had previously suspected. I was out of the woods. What a relief . . . and what a miracle! My husband and all three children arrived in the hospital, and my husband gratefully noted that a twenty-four-hour storm in our lives had passed.

Although I needed a month to fully recover from this incident, I knew I had been given a second chance to live. I realized that life was fragile, and that sometimes I did need to ask for help.

I also realized that I had spent my life up to that point collecting things, love, and wisdom. I vowed to use the rest of my life, with which I had been blessed, to give back to society all that I had received.

16

"Keep the Bond and Always Stick Together"

Manisha was in her last year of medical school at Cornell University in Manhattan. We visited her frequently. One day she asked her father if he was prepared to have his own doctor and stop treating himself. She had raised this question for at least three years, since beginning medical school. Each time Viren had an excuse: first Kapila's graduation from high school, then Manisha's wedding. It was clear to me that deep down in his heart he knew that if he went for a full checkup, he might end up having a cardiac by-pass. Viren has a strong family history of hypertension. One of his closest uncles passed away because of brain hemorrhage secondary to hypertension. His father, mother, and eldest brother also suffered from hypertension. Viren, who is a cardiologist, had self-diagnosed hypertension, but he believed it was labile and he did not need medical treatment.

Manisha was persistent. All the excuses he gave for postponing his full checkup had been used and there were no more he could offer. So, in an irritable tone, he told her to find a cardiologist. Manisha went straight to Dr. Hayes, the chairman of the department of medicine, who was a cardiologist but close to retirement and not accepting any new patients. However, when he learned that this patient was her father, he readily agreed to see him.

Viren arrived for his first visit. The full exam and electrocardiogram were normal. Dr. Hayes suggested that a thallium stress test would be helpful to rule out any coronary heart disease, especially because he had a strong family history.

As Viren was undergoing the thallium stress test, he noticed that the monitor was showing changes. He knew this meant that the test had to stop.

All the doctors involved in his case suggested that he must have a cardiac catheterization. It was scheduled in a day because by now they were all aware that he was Manisha's dad.

Early the next morning, Manisha, her husband Raj, Viral, and I accompanied Viren to the hospital for the cardiac catheterization. Kapila came down from Yale and joined us at the hospital. When the test was completed, his cardiac surgeon, Dr. Krieger, sat us all down and explained that Viren had multiple blockages in arteries that supply blood to the heart and he would need a quadruple bypass, which is open heart surgery. Viren needed to be in the hospital right away and surgery was scheduled for forty-eight hours later.

Manisha, Raj, Kapila, Viral, and I accompanied him to the operating room as he was being rolled along on a stretcher. The nurse's aide stopped the stretcher for a minute as the operating room's automatic door opened. We could not accompany him beyond this point. We all kissed him good luck with tears in our eyes. He said to us, "Keep the bond and always stick together."

This was the hardest moment of my life. The uncertainty of the outcome of major heart surgery caused tremendous fear and anxiety. We were told that he would be in the operating room for at least eight hours. I told everyone to get their work done while I waited in the visiting area outside the intensive care unit where he would be taken after the surgery; we would all get together again then. I promised to keep them updated if I heard anything from his doctors. It was April 8, 2008. Viral was scheduled to take SAT exams. Kapila's final exams were fast approaching. Manisha would graduate from medical school at the end of May. It was a busy time for our family.

After eight hours we saw Viren coming out from the operating room, sedated but making sounds suggestive of pain. We were allowed to visit him in the intensive care unit one by one and stay for just a few minutes. I was concerned and could not bear to see him in so much pain. The doctors had called several consultants but we did not know the reason why they were all surrounding his bed. Then we learned that he was bleeding inside his chest and they were trying to find where the bleeding was coming from. Finally a decision was made to take him back into the operating room and open up his chest to find and fix the problem. This was devastating news. But we were helpless. A few hours passed and finally I saw him again, in deep sedation but comfortable. The doctors told us to go home as he was stable.

That night everything that had occurred from the time Viren saw a cardiologist went through my mind. I was amazed to see that Manisha had taken charge of making decisions since she saw I could not do it; my judgment was derailed. I was not an objective physician in this situation but rather an emotionally shaken-up wife. I had told the others that I trusted her judgment. In every discussion leading up to the surgery, I noticed that Raj supported her every move and Kapila and Viral chimed in with their questions. Everyone had full trust in her.

The worst was over, and Viren was making progress. It all ended well. I have reflected on this experience and realized that because Manisha knew about Viren's family medical history, she took a bold step to get her father appropriate medical attention. She communicated effectively with all of us and convinced everyone, including Viren, that he needed this intervention. She answered Kapila's and Viral's incessant questions about the heart surgery with accuracy and hope. We all had faith in her. Viren had taught our family the value of staying together; in trusting each other's decisions, we would overcome any trials and tribulations of life. In this situation, our family stuck together and was able to withstand a major storm in our lives.

17

A Sudden Grievous Loss

Nalini and her Sister Niru in their teenage years

W henever I hear the Hindi song, *"Lag ja gale,"* I
am immediately transported back to the night of
July 24, 2000: the most horrific night of my life.

A few days earlier, my younger sister Niru, her husband,
Kirit, and her fifteen-year-old daughter, Bhumi, had flown
to London, England. They lived in New York and were to
embark on a two-week tour of Europe the next morning.
They had spent a few days in London with our dear cousin
from India, Manju.

July 22, 2000 was a happy day for Niru. She and her
family and Manju had all gone out shopping for a dress for
Bhumi, who was going to celebrate her sixteenth birthday
a month after they returned to New York. My sister had
planned a gala sweet-sixteen party. But Bhumi was having
the hardest time finding a dress just right for the occasion.
She had not succeeded in finding one in New York before
they left for London.

After a whole day of browsing from one shop to another,
Bhumi saw a dress, peacock blue with sequined embroidery.
It was love at first sight. She went into the dressing room
and came out in this gorgeous dress, beaming. Niru was
delighted: she took pictures from all angles. She said to
Bhumi, "I feel like I am at your sweet-sixteen party today."

They all went back to the hotel talking about the
wonderful day they had spent shopping. They started to
watch a movie at 8.00 pm, but an hour later Niru said,
"I will take a shower so that in the morning everyone is
not rushed in the bathroom. Anyway, I have a throbbing
headache. I have already taken painkillers; maybe a hot
shower will help." Everyone was tired, and one by one they
all dozed off.

Manju woke up around 2.00 am. Niru was not in the
room. The last time Manju had seen her, Niru had gone to
take a shower in the bathroom. The bathroom lights were

on, and the door was locked. Manju knocked, but there was no answer. Her heart started to beat fast. She woke up Kirit and called the hotel operator. Within minutes, security guards had broken open the bathroom door. There lay Niru on the floor with a tiny bruise near her lips. She had showered and was dressed in her pajamas. They could not tell what had happened. Niru did not respond to touch, sound, or even painful stimuli. They rushed to call an ambulance and followed the ambulance in a cab.

I received a frantic phone call from Manju, and my mother and I left New York for London on the next available flight. While in the air, my feelings fluctuated between my fear and grief as a sister and my thoughts and assessments as a physician. I was very afraid to acknowledge my suspicion that Niru could be in a coma.

When I arrived in London, Manju told me what had happened on the way to the hospital:

"Three of us sat in the cab, which was following the ambulance carrying Niru. I was holding Bhumi's hand as we sat in the rear seat, and Kirit sat in the front seat next to the cab driver.

The cab driver was an Indian guy. A Hindi song was playing on his radio. The song had beautiful lyrics: "*Lag ja gale ke phir ye hasin raat ho na ho . . . shayad phir whohi mulakat ho na ho*" ("Hug me tight because I don't know if this night will ever come back again . . . I don't know if our union will ever occur again"). My heart was throbbing, and I asked myself whether this song was meaningful to the event that had just occurred.

The ambulance arrived at the hospital. We all rushed out, paid the cab driver, and thanked him for rushing and keeping pace with the ambulance. I said to him in Hindi, 'The song that played through the car ride made me tearful.' He wished us luck."

129

Manju's description of everything that had happened before I got to London was so vivid that I felt as if I had been with her throughout these events.

When I arrived at the hospital, we waited outside the intensive care unit where Niru was being treated. We were all engrossed in our own thoughts. There was pin-drop silence, but being a physician, I could not deny my suspicion that we might receive some horrific news from the doctors. My mind zigzagged from being an objective physician and an emotionally invested older sister.

The doctors did a repeat MRI of the brain and allowed me to stay with my sister throughout the test. It was hard for me to keep my usual neutral and professional stance. This was my younger sister. We were just the two of us; we had no other siblings. Niru looked up to me in everything in life. Just five years older, I was her caretaker, her mother-figure, as well as her friend and confidante.

As I watched the MRI showing all parts of Niru's brain covered with blood, I suspected that she had had a brain aneurysm that bled. She was placed on a ventilator as I sat there, watching her blood pressure fluctuate rapidly.

The doctor told us that the next morning another doctor would come, and they would try to remove the ventilator. If Niru was able to breathe on her own, then there would be hope for her survival. We were all speechless and could hardly comprehend what was going on.

Every few minutes, we hugged Niru, tears dropping from our eyes, and that song from the cab driver's radio continued to ring in my ears: "Hug me tight because I don't know if this night will ever come back again . . . I don't know if our union will ever occur again."

The next morning, two doctors took my sister off the ventilator, and she was not able to breathe on her own. We had to let her go.

Was that song sending us a message and preparing us for what was soon to be a reality? We will never know. As she departed from this world, Niru's organs were donated to seven people in London. The only consolation we had was that Niru lives on through the lives of those seven people.

Prayers after Niru passed: observing and praying are Nalini, Jain monk
Shilapiji, mother Sushila, cousin Manju, and another Jain monk

Nonverbal communication between Bhumi and her mom, Niru

18

The Fire of 2012

On January 26, 2012, at the end of a three-week visit to India, I was celebrating my sixty-sixth birthday with a small group of relatives and friends. Viren called to wish me a happy birthday. His voice was rather soft and mellow. I could tell that he had something on his mind that he was hiding from me.

He was trying to hide from me the dreadful news that on January 24, 2012, our house had caught fire. We had been installing a generator for the house as a source of back-up power. Two licensed electricians were on the premises running a test. While running the test, an electrician had crossed the wires, which led 220-volt electricity to surge through the entire house, causing an electrical fire in our master bedroom.

Viren was at work, and my eighty-six-year-old mother and our housekeeper were at home. While the electricians were running the test, my mother smelled something burning. She alerted our housekeeper who saw smoke coming out of our bedroom. My mother and housekeeper got out of the house and called Viren, and the electricians called the fire department. Fortunately, everyone in the family was safe.

By the time Viren reached home, the area surrounding our house looked like a war zone. The fire department had arrived and had used a massive amount of water to put out the fire. They had broken all of the windows and thrown furniture down into the yard to allow the heat of the fire to escape. As a result of the fire itself and the water used by the fire department, one-half of the house was destroyed, from the ceiling to the floor.

Viren did the preliminary work with the help of our daughter Kapila and tried not to give me the dreadful news while I was in India. However, I knew that something was horribly wrong and pushed him to tell me what it was. When Viren finally explained, I was in shock. I did not know what I would find when I returned home two days later. I was overtaken by an exceptional feeling of grief as I imagined an unfathomable amount of loss.

I tried to compose myself. A lesson from the Hindu scripture, the Bhagavad Gita, came into my mind:

> What have you lost that you are crying?
> What did you come with that you have lost?
> What did you create that was destroyed?
> Whatever you have was obtained from here.
> Whatever you have was given right here.
> What belongs to you today will be someone else's
>   tomorrow.
> And will belong to someone else the day after
>   tomorrow.
> Creation, destruction and re-creation is the basic
>   law of the universe.

I shared the shocking news of the fire with my relatives and friends in India. They were surprised that my spiritual thinking had helped me to compose myself. I was now more concerned that Viren had to deal with this traumatic event alone, in my absence.

I returned home four days after the fire had taken place. Viren and I went straight from the airport to our house. All of our belongings, memorabilia, books, important documents, and mundane intimate objects had been destroyed. Both of us stared at the black soot-covered remains of our bedroom, which could hardly be recognized. We were heartbroken as the reality of what had happened set in.

Forty-two years earlier, we had arrived in the United States with no belongings. In the years since then, we made a life for ourselves and our children. After the fire, we felt as if we would be starting all over again. We realized that we were not in our twenties any more. We had less energy. We had thought that it was time to enjoy what we had built over all these years. But a higher power had something else in mind for us.

After staying with our daughter Kapila and her family for a few days, we were placed in an apartment by our homeowners' insurance company. After living in a house for thirty-four years, with plenty of space and convenient access from driveway to kitchen, we had forgotten what apartment life was like.

Our next task was to identify and inventory all of our belongings that had been destroyed, so that the agency hired by our insurance company could discard and dispose of them. As we walked through the place with our daughters, labeling and identifying everything, I felt as though I were identifying dead bodies in a war zone.

Manisha pointed out the irony that right outside the master bedroom, where the fire had started, was a portable fire extinguisher, still intact. We had placed a fire extinguisher on each floor of the house as a preventive measure, but to no avail.

Among the soot-covered remains, I found a ceramic plaque with the framed handprints of our son, Viral, that he had made when he was five years old. It had been hanging on a wall in our bedroom. I brushed off the soot and cleaned the plaque. It was totally intact. I felt euphoric; at least one intimate object full of cherished memories had survived!

Over the next six months, our lives were completely changed, but we continued living life, going to work, and planning for the future. Viral's wedding was planned to be held only three months after the fire. It is said that every cloud has a silver lining; this was certainly true for us. All of the Indian clothing, matching Indian jewelry, and Indian paraphernalia that we needed for his traditional Indian wedding were in the suitcase I had brought back from India. In addition, before leaving for India, I had begun packing other wedding items, such as gifts for the bride and her family, in a separate room, which was untouched by the fire. Therefore, everything we needed for the marriage celebration was still intact. The last-minute preparations for the wedding took our minds off of the destruction and reconstruction that was going on at our home, and we thoroughly enjoyed the picture-perfect occasion.

This incredibly trying experience helped us learn many life lessons. We were touched by the emotional support we received from our children and our friends, which gave us the strength to start anew. We knew that we were not alone. Rebuilding our house required us to deal with insurance agents, town personnel, utility companies, and contractors. Our experiences with each one of them were challenging in their own way. We laughed and cried as we progressed through the reconstruction process.

Another silver lining of the fire was our excitement as we set out to buy everything new, from tiles to furniture.

The process was exhausting, but I enjoyed shopping and looked forward to having a modern home. Though we were not simply relishing the life that we had built over the years, as we had expected, we were able to enjoy the process of rebuilding our home to suit our current needs. We were also able to rebuild our lives with fewer belongings, since now we truly understand the lesson from the Bhagavad Gita that we need to learn to let go of our material possessions because what we own today will be someone else's tomorrow.

19

Pearls of Wisdom

I have always tried to share with my children the pearls of wisdom, big and small, that I have acquired throughout my life, from my own experiences and from the many wise people I have known. Therefore, when writing this book, I invited all three of my children to help me compile the pearls of wisdom that have been meaningful to them.

I offer these pearls of wisdom for you to read slowly, think about deeply, reflect upon often, return to, expand upon, and pass on.

1. Think positively. The more you purge negative thinking from your mind, the more you make room for positive thinking to come in.
2. When we are young, we have a lot of time and energy, but little money. When we are middle-aged, we may have energy and some money, but very little time. When we are old, we may have time and some money, but little energy. Make the best use of what you have when you have it.
3. Gratitude is the biggest virtue. Find at least one thing to be grateful for every day.
4. Happiness and unhappiness are based on one's expectations.

5. Compete with yourself. Aim to be better every day in all aspects of life.

6. Everyone makes mistakes. Instead of brooding over your mistakes, learn lessons and do not make the same mistakes again.

7. Life is too short to make all the mistakes. Learn from the mistakes of others.

8. In life, there are some people whom you may see every day but never grow closer to. There are others whom you may go a long time without seeing, but when you do, it is like nothing ever changed. Invest your time and energy in the latter.

9. Embrace change in life. There is nothing permanent except change. Every phase of life has its own charm.

10. You cannot change other people. You can only change what you expect of them and how you react to them.

11. There are always people who have more than you and people who have less than you. Be grateful for what you have, and don't dwell on what you don't.

12. Tell stories about your families. Those who know a lot about the trials and tribulations of their families tend to cope better when they face challenges.

13. Be proud of your heritage. Have a strong intergenerational bond.

14. Preserve your core values while embracing new progress.

15. Reflect upon your past to learn from it and to build a progressive future.

16. When seeking a partner in life, the most important thing is that you share common values.

17. Your spouse's cooking is the best food in the world. Never be critical when your partner tries to do something for you.

18. Effective communication is essential to having a happy family.
19. Be good team players as a couple. Your spouse will be a team player in the household as well as in work life if you accept his/her contribution without criticism.
20. As parents, try not to disagree or contradict one another in front of the children. Present a united front and work out disagreements behind closed doors. Children will set up one parent against the other to get what they want.
21. The best heritage you can give your child is values and morals.
22. Educate your children. Help your children graduate without any debt. You will have given them the best tools to grow further.
23. Test your children's maturity and ability to use money wisely before putting money in their hands.
24. Identify the strengths and weaknesses of your children and build on their strengths.
25. Teach children the value of hard work to earn money. Parents have a responsibility to provide for their basic needs. Luxuries should be earned by children.
26. Applaud and praise in public and give negative feedback and criticism in private.
27. When leaving any place, always turn around and ask yourself, "Did I forget anything?"
28. Never carry credit card debt. Purchase what you need by credit card and pay off the credit card bills in full every month.
29. Shop thoughtfully. Do not hoard things just because you like them. Before you buy anything, ask yourself: Do I need it? Is it worth the price? Can I afford it?

30. Give your discards to charities such as Veterans of America or the Big Brother Big Sister program. One person's discards can be another person's treasure.

Epilogue

We all seek our purpose in life. Most of us wonder how we can make a positive difference during our brief time on this earth. It is not the date of one's birth or the date of one's departure that really matters. What matters is the "dash" between those two years and what was done during that time.

Viren and I are so fortunate to have had the life together that we have. We have worked as a team at home and at work for forty-three years of marriage. All our wishes and ambitions to succeed professionally, travel, and raise a family have been fulfilled.

Our honeymoon continues as we move on to the next phase of our lives. This includes contributing to religious and spiritual activities here in the United States and supporting non-governmental organizations in India that work to empower women and provide education and vocational training to children in rural areas. In addition, I have helped provide medical services in some of the most remote villages in India. Since Viren and I have received more than we ever asked for, we now work as a team to give back to society.

Appendix

At three different stages of my life, each of my adult children decided to interview me to learn more about my life experiences. Some of the material that emerged during these interviews has been part of other chapters, and I apologize for some repetition. These interviews meant a lot to me because they were conducted one-on-one, free-flowing and unrehearsed. My children asked questions that elicited some of my most tightly held thoughts. These interviews also reveal my children's unique perspectives about my life and our family.

Interview I: Viral

Viral on his first birthday

Nine years ago, while passing by the Story Corps Booth at Grand Central station in New York, I was impressed by what Story Corps was doing. This organization collects stories of people all over the country and stores them in the Library of Congress; participants receive a CD of their interview to pass on to generations to come. Viral and I discussed Story Corps' mission and decided to visit the Story Corps booth at Grand Central station where he interviewed me.

Viral:
Hi. My name is Viral Juthani. I am twenty-three years old. And today is March 18, 2005. We are in Grand Central Terminal in New York City at the Story Corp booth which collects stories of people in the USA. And I am going to be interviewing my mother.

Nalini:
And my name is Nalini Juthani. I am fifty-nine years old, and I'm going to be interviewed by my son, Viral.

Viral:
I wanted to start close to the beginning and see if you can tell me a little bit about what it was like growing up in India.

Nalini:
First of all, I grew up in India in a middle-class family. My father died when I was five years old, and I do not remember much before that, but I do have a memory of him asking somebody to bring peaches from the store because I loved peaches and he wanted to feed me peaches with his own hands.

After my father passed away, I grew up with my mother, who, as a widow, never got remarried even though she was only twenty-four years old when my father passed. My sister was born approximately six months after his death.

So growing up, I saw the resiliency of my mother and how she raised both of us with the help of her parents.

My grandmother became my key person, because she encouraged my mother to participate in all kinds of religious activities to occupy her mind. My grandmother took care of us, because she mostly stayed at home.

One of the things that I carried with me growing up was that my grandfather always stressed the importance of education. And in India he used to recommend that I subscribe to *Reader's Digest* and to all kinds of medical journals, which cost a lot of money at the time, especially in *rupees* (Indian currency). He thought that I should be spending more time reading even though I was more interested in painting and doing creative activities. But that stress on education stayed with me.

On the other hand, my grandmother was the one who provided most of the care and love. In those days, people used to do a lot of knitting, and she was well-versed at that. She used to make one analogy that I will never forget, that life is like a tangled ball of yarn. "Look at the yarn when you get it. You'll find that there are two ends of the yarn. If you pull the wrong end, you will find that the entire ball will become even more tightly tangled. If you pull the right one, it will untangle smoothly, and you will be able to make use of all the yarn without a problem."

Although I didn't quite understand the message at the time, I always liked to listen to older people, because I thought that they had a tremendous amount of wisdom. And they used to love me because many young people did not want to listen to them.

However, as I grew older, I was able to relate back to those incidents and my grandmother's analogy. When confronting a problem, I would consider the ball of yarn. If you can analyze a problem carefully by talking more, collecting more data, learning more about it without becoming judgmental, then you can identify two sides of an issue which would be equivalent to the two ends of the ball, and be able to maneuver it more effectively. If you find that the strand from the ball of yarn is stuck and is not moving, realize that you made a mistake, learn from it, and take the corrective steps. I thought about this analogy a lot in my childhood.

Viral:
Can you tell me the story of feeding the poor, homeless kids at the bottom of your building?

Nalini:
Sure. As I was growing up, there were a lot of homeless children outside our apartment building, and they used to eat out of garbage pails. So every night, at the end of dinner, I would put whatever food was left over in a large pan and take it downstairs. The children would come over, and I would feed them. And that food was certainly better than the food they took out of the garbage pail.

During the mango season, when mangos were fresh and very expensive, I would not eat the mangos that my family served until I had fed the homeless children. My family used to get very annoyed because they wanted me to eat the mangos, but I refused until *my children* as I called them, had the mangos first.

And lastly, on my birthday, I always used to take them all to a store that sold chocolates and pastries. Nobody wanted to ever see these people because they were homeless and they were always begging. But this time they would come with me, and they would all form an organized line. And one by one, they came up to the counter, and I would tell the store owner, give these people whatever they want, and I'm going to pay for the whole thing. They were treated with respect, they behaved in a disciplined manner, and I paid for their treat. That was a gift to me on my birthdays. And that was a very special time.

Viral:
How old were you at that time?

Nalini:
I was between the ages of sixteen and twenty.

Viral:
So now, why don't you tell me what it was like for you to arrive in the United States as an immigrant, and what were your dreams?

Nalini:
It was June 28, 1970, when your dad and I arrived in New York City for just a few days and then went on to Michigan. In Michigan, we stayed in a town called Highland Park. This was the first time that we had gone away from home for a very long stay. We had already finished medical school in India, and we were going to pursue graduate medical education in this country.

Dad already had an internship in Michigan, and I was going to wait until I could acquire all the credentials to start an internship in the United States.

Coming as an immigrant was an exciting and challenging experience. When you have never been in a country 10,000 miles away from home and have nobody in the country that you can call family, life is very different.

The first thing your dad and I wanted to do was to collect one thousand dollars, so that if there were any problems, we could go back home. So those one thousand dollars, we put away for good.

And then we had the dreams of enhancing our education and practicing here and at some point have our own family. For a while we had thought we would return to India and practice there, but that thought only lasted a short time. We realized that this is where we wanted to stay, and we were going to have a lot of meaningful experiences here and raise our children here.

Viral:
What did it feel like when you came to the realization that you weren't going back home?

Nalini:
It was a mixed feeling, because on one hand, when you come to another country, there is a tremendous sense of loss, a loss of the familiarity of a home environment, loss of friends, and loss of family. The United States also had a very heterogeneous population, unlike India where everyone is more or less the same. This took some adjusting.

And so it was quite a bit of cultural challenge. And this challenge became ultimately my interest. This is the field of study I pursued within psychiatry after I had started my residency training.

Viral:
So what would you say were the keys to your success in your professional life, and what lessons have you learned from your experiences?

Nalini:
This is a huge question. People tell me that I have been very successful in the United States. I have bought into

this compliment. First, the initial challenges that I faced in my educational experiences in this country were very interesting.

I decided that both of us, my husband and I being doctors, were not going to go through life being on call every other night. I was not going to be in a new country and have no idea what the country is like. I did not want to just wake up in the morning, go to the hospital, come home, and go to sleep.

So I decided that I wasn't going to practice medicine, and I didn't for the first five years. During this time, I met very interesting people, which is something that I always enjoyed doing, and I took all kinds of paramedical nine-to-five jobs. I worked as a medical librarian and as an operating room (OR) technician; I worked in a clinic, which I did not know was an illegally operated abortion clinic until one day I went to work and the clinic was vacated without notice.

Then I worked as a laboratory technician, so I did all kinds of paramedical jobs. Doing these jobs got me to see the medical field from a very different point of view. And when I started my own training, I was way ahead of my immigrant colleagues because I had worked with people in America from various fields and various cultures. I met people who were immigrants and those who had been in this country for three to four generations. I learned about various cultures and traditions. My co-workers visited my home and I visited theirs. We exchanged stories from our traditions. This exposure helped me make friends from various backgrounds, not just from my own.

It also helped me communicate better with nurses who did not always respect new immigrant doctors. Patients too did not offer the kind of respect we were used to receiving in India. Patients would address us as "Hey, you, doc," which was not the respectful way to address doctors we were used to. I learned about slang people used in daily communication. My chairman of the department once said to me, "I always thought you were different from the other residents we had and I wondered if you were born here."

By the time I started my residency, we had moved to New York and our home life was already somewhat settled. Your oldest sister, Manisha, was already born. Since Dad had completed his residency, he had more free time; he was able to help me in raising Manisha.

I always felt that having such a helpful partner in life is extremely necessary to achieving success, especially if you are a woman. I came from a culture where I was taught that being a good wife, keeping a house, and being a mother are the most important things in life for a woman, and that education and profession are definitely secondary. Those things are the icing on the cake, and you've got to do them on the side. So quickly I realized that I was doing two full-time jobs.

But success is not just earning money. Success is multifaceted. Some believe that success means earning a lot of money. Some believe that successful people have a lot of prestige and the power that goes along with it. I believe that success includes all of those things and more.

In my field of psychiatry, you really get to understand people not just from their outside but also from their inside, which includes the mind, the emotions, and the spirit. I felt that I was able to make a difference in the lives of the people I treated. Having empathy, that listening ear, is another thing that helped me become more understanding of people and what they go through. And I think that attribute has helped me professionally and personally. In my academic career I became a clinical professor at Albert Einstein College of Medicine and the assistant dean for students at Bronx Lebanon Hospital. I had a successful and fulfilling academic career.

Having children (and we have three) was another highly educational experience, because I always thought that I learned a lot from my own children. And I was never a perfect mother, but I knew that I was better every time I learned something from my children. And I think that is another facet of success in life.

So I think learning from everyone, learning from every human being, is the key to success in life.

Viral:
I can say from firsthand experience that you've done a spectacular job balancing both areas of your life. Can you tell me what I was like as a baby and a young child?

Nalini:
You are the youngest of our family. Our oldest child, Manisha, and you are eight years apart. We had Manisha before I started working in psychiatry. After she was born, I was able to start my psychiatry residency, and then we had Kapi. So Manisha and Kapi are five years apart. After Kapi was born, I did my board exams, and then we planned to have you.

So you were very much planned. In fact, a book was written on ways to select the sex of your child, a book that many people have used. I discussed the book with my obstetrician, and he said I had nothing to lose and that given how obsessive I was, I might succeed. And we did.

And sure enough, when the amniocentesis was done, they asked if we wanted to know the sex of our child. We said yes. And then we knew that you were a boy. And I must say that feeling at the time was of sheer joy. All our children brought happiness, but if somebody can distinguish between happiness and joy, you brought tremendous joy. In many Indian cultures, having a son is considered very desirable. Daddy and I both wanted to have both boys and girls.

As a baby, you only smiled and laughed. I never noticed your gymnastics ability until you were about nine months old. One day, I was tossing you up and down as many people do, and you somersaulted in the air and landed on the floor on the opposite side of me. And I looked up and said, where did my child go? You had landed on the other side and developed a greenstick fracture in your thigh.

So that was a scary experience, but on the bright side, some of the best pictures we have are from that time. As a child, you had curly hair. And when we did the head-shaving ceremony when you were one year old, those curly locks never came back. When you were born, you had a unique personality and this continued into childhood. You were a charmer from the time you were born. And those are my memories of you as a baby.

As a young boy you acted like a clown. You played karate and you were constantly kicking things. I thought that you would become a martial artist because you kicked everything; I never knew that you would become a doctor.

Viral:
What advice would you give me about raising my own children?

Nalini:
First, to remember that children are brought in this world by the choice of parents.

Second, children have to be raised; they can't just grow up. To make an analogy; we raise flowers, we raise fruits, we raise vegetables, and we have a garden. Weeds just grow and all they need is water and sunlight. Children should never be treated like weeds, because they will grow up if necessary. But to fulfill their potential, children have to be raised. And that's the second thing to always keep in mind.

Third, children want one thing in life, and that is "my way." And as long as they get their way, there's no problem. With you being a professional—and maybe your wife will be a professional as well—your challenge in raising your kids will not be in giving them money but in giving them values. To do that, you need to put in the time, money, and energy. And that energy must come from both the parents. It cannot be done by just one.

When I was raising you guys, I thought I should get caretakers who were highly intelligent, because then they would introduce intelligent ways of playing with the children. I learned that I was wrong. You need caretakers who are loving and who put the children before themselves.

Does love translate into giving children what they want? No. Love translates into nurturing and teaching. And all parents have to become teachers. Teaching your kids the values of life, how to become a good human being, is the most important thing. Everything else will come on the side.

In the process, you will find that your kids will sometimes be unhappy with you. And that is really painful because you don't want to see your kids' faces go down. But talk to the kids; explain to them what you are doing. Always remember that kids may not like what you are saying to them at that moment, but somehow they register it in the back of their minds. I see those values coming out with your sisters now as they are raising their own kids.

Viral:
What's the most valuable lesson you can share with a budding doctor like me?

159

Nalini:

The medical profession is a dynamic profession. Things change every day. Things that were going on when I was going through medical school and practicing medicine are very different today. However, there is something that always will remain constant: there will always be somebody who is suffering and there will always be somebody who can help them and relieve them from that suffering. That's the doctor—and one should never underestimate that bond between a doctor and a patient.

When I was doing my training, the words "client" and "provider" never existed. They're hard for me to even accept at this time because there is a difference between a client/provider relationship and a doctor/patient relationship. The doctor goes beyond his own interest, his own life, and will often sacrifice his own interest for the sake and the betterment of the patient. A client and a provider have a business relationship. These are two very different relationships.

I hope that if you have to use those words, you'll use them for the sake of semantics, so the culture around you will understand, but that deep down in your heart you will always remember this is a profession where you have to completely give yourself, because it is truly a privilege to be a physician. There are a lot of people who would like to do these things, but this profession is not given to them. And I always felt that this is an ability that was given to me by a higher power, and I will use it for the betterment of others.

So if you keep that in mind, the rest will fall into place. And is money important? Yes, it's important. Is going out and doing charitable work important? Yes, that is also very important. The most important thing is how to keep a balance so that greed does not take over in the doctor/patient relationship.

Viral:
Tell me one memorable story that shows the importance of the doctor/patient relationship.

Nalini:
The doctor-patient relationship is very special to me. I once treated a woman who had dissociative identity disorder, also known as multiple personality disorder. I treated her for four years. Eventually she came to terms with her condition and accepted all the different personalities she had. Each one of these personalities had a different psychiatric illness. So it was almost like treating a depressed person, a mood-disordered person, a psychotic person, and a very anxious person all in one body. The depressed person was always trying to kill herself and the mood-disordered person was always trying to find the next attractive guy to sleep with, so obviously this was a very challenging patient to treat.

At the end of the four years, as she was progressing well, we gradually tapered off her treatment and she did extremely well. Throughout the subsequent years, every now and then, people from the hospital said to me, "You know, your patient was talking about you and wanted to say hello" or "I saw her in the church" or "I saw her in the store and she wanted to say hi." And because she did not live that far away, I always wondered why she was sending me messages but not ever calling me.

So I called her, and she said, "I must tell you the truth. This relationship between doctor and patient is so unique and special to me. I feel that one day I might call and somebody will say, 'She doesn't work here anymore.' And that would be such a sad day for me, so I can't bear to call. I would rather send messages with other people and hear from them that you are doing well. "Once my doctor, you are my doctor forever, and wherever I go, you will always be my doctor."

I think that is a short story of the importance of that doctor-patient relationship.

Viral:
What's your dream for me in my career?

Nalini:
Every time you ask this question, I find it emotionally charged, the reason being I always have high dreams for all my children, but especially for you, because I always felt you are a very special soul. This is beyond what Daddy and I have contributed to because the souls arrive to us, and it is a blessing to us. That soul has the capacity to do a lot and will not be confined to the day-to-day routine.

And my dream is that you will be a very good doctor. And I have some evidence to base that on. An older lady with whom you talked for a few minutes told me, "I want to live long enough so that I can call him my doctor." That's a very special thing that any human being can tell a doctor, that this is my doctor. And she had had only a short encounter with you. But in the future, I think you will touch many human beings, and you will do things not only in the United States but also abroad. I think you may reach out to some of the people who do not have access to medical care because of their situations. I also think that you will become a wonderful father and a terrific husband.

And that's my dream, that the generations that follow will be contributors to this Juthani family tree, will pass on this value system and add to it.

Viral:
How would you say you would like to be remembered?

Nalini:

I would like to be remembered as a woman who was able to overcome the constraints placed by society on women. I think most women, regardless of their ethnicity or heritage, went through similar things. I have risked many things to travel the road less traveled and left a trail behind.

I have always been an innovative person. I take challenges, and I get things done. I was the first medical student from my university to leave without completing the final three months of internship in India and received permission to complete it abroad. After me, many more women were able to do that. I actually met a woman who told me that she did the same thing because some woman named Nalini had done it before, and it turned out that she was talking about me!

I would love for young women, when confronted with personal and professional challenges, to look back at me and say, "Look what she was able to do." I hope that my experiences and ability to balance my personal and professional lives can remind those women of what is possible and what they are capable of.

Education has been my mission and has been at the core of everything I have done. I feel that when people don't do the right thing, it is because they don't know better. And I've always taken the position that it is my responsibility to educate them, whether it is in a professional setting or in life in general. I want to be remembered as a person who was an educator, an educator of life.

Viral:

Well, it's a privilege and an honor to talk to you. And luckily, I've had that privilege my whole life because I'm your son. So thank you again.

Baby Viral loved being bounced in the air by Nalini

Viral in elementary school

Viral receiving medical diploma from the dean
of Yale University Medical School

Viral and Rupa after their wedding ceremony in 2012

Interview II: Manisha

Manisha and Raj with Ishani, Shaan, and their first dog, Misty

My daughter, Manisha, is a doctor and a mother as well as being my oldest child, and she is very much like me. She has been an educator, and most recently she was appointed director of the infectious disease training program at Yale University Medical School. I was very happy that she too wanted to interview me as I was writing this book.

Manisha:
You were a trend setter in your time. Can you give some examples of the courage and confidence you had that led to success in your academic career?

Nalini:
I did not start out knowing that I can be a trend-setter. Others have described me as one when they've heard my stories, but I've realized that being a trendsetter has fulfilled me in life. I truly feel that women can do anything and should have the courage to follow their dreams to fulfill themselves. I have never accepted the status quo, and I would encourage women to push limits and have the courage to be different. And when you are different, half of those around you will accept you and half will not. Look out for the greater good. If you can convince yourself that you are doing something for more than a self-serving purpose, you will be able to make the difference that you are looking for.

I can think of three examples when I feel that I showed this courage.

More than a decade ago, I was nominated to the American Psychiatric Association's (APA) task force on strategic planning by the Board of Trustees. I observed that committee members didn't share their views openly because they were afraid of how they would be perceived by other members. For decades, all former presidents of the APA had been invited to Board of Trustees meetings, a costly and inefficient expense for the organization. I proposed that only the last two past presidents should be invited. Other members appreciated this idea, and ultimately the motion was passed. Some members of the Board of Trustees never expected that this motion would pass. Others mentioned to me that although they had supported my proposal, they hadn't had the courage to make such a motion themselves. But I accepted my appointment with only one goal in mind: how can I make a difference? With this mindset, I was willing to take risks that others were unwilling to take.

At Bronx Lebanon Hospital, our Child Psychiatry program wanted to be part of the academic aspects of Albert Einstein College of Medicine (AECOM). To further our academic affiliation and participation, our faculty and director of our department wanted to start a child psychiatry fellowship. In our monthly executive meeting I presented to the chairman of AECOM and the executive committee our desire to start such a fellowship. The chairman of psychiatry at AECOM asked in a condescending tone, "How do you expect to recruit fellows?" The undertone to his question was, "Who would want to go to Bronx Lebanon Hospital?" I was quick to answer, "Currently fifty percent of our graduating residents go to outside child psychiatry programs. I feel very confident that given the opportunity to have a fellowship program at our site, we would recruit our own graduates." The director of our department was surprised by my quick and positive response, and the executive committee and chairman accepted our proposal.

When I was on the executive committee of the American Association of Directors of Psychiatry Residency Training

(AADPRT), my colleague and I were given the task of exploring why there was rapid turnover of program directors. We took it upon ourselves to conduct a survey of the program directors all over the country. Most of them were concerned about being vocal. However, on the written survey, a majority of respondents said that their hospital administrations were not providing them with adequate administrative support to run a program. They were very frustrated and felt pulled in a variety of directions. When I presented the findings of this survey, the directors of training were able to share the findings with their hospital administrations.

Manisha:
What advice would you give to younger professional women who are trying to balance a career and raising a family?

Nalini:
My experiences are over thirty years old, but there are still some common themes. First, the culture here is very different from that of India. People raised here will naturally share family responsibilities with their spouses. Accept your spouse's contributions whatever they are. Don't force him to do things that are not within his comfort zone, but accept whatever he is willing to do. Second, as a working mother, my biggest concern was to look out for the welfare of my kids. I advise women to spend money on hiring childcare workers and housekeepers who will help with daily household chores. When you come home, you should be able to spend time with your children, husband, and family. Third, I've always been a micro-manager and there are positive aspects to that attribute. But in hindsight, I've learned to look at the forest and not the trees. I would encourage young micro-managers to keep this in mind.

Manisha:
As you approach seventy, do you feel like you are getting old?

Nalini:
Physically, I don't look my age because Indian skin ages slowly. Aging is a process that involves the body, the mind and the spirit. Physically, I realize that I am slowing down, but people say that my slower version is still faster than most others. Emotionally, I feel that I've become more tolerant, patient, introspective, and forgiving. Spiritually, I have recognized that the connections we develop in life are short-lived and are broken by losses (death or moving away) or people are changing priorities. This can lead to loneliness. Some of our relationships are need-based and these don't always last, while others are a connection of souls. When we lose our soul mates, those relationships can't be replaced. "It is not easy to get old," a wise woman once told me.

Once again, I feel that my innovative and creative ideas are emerging. I look forward to making the next phase of life more meaningful and fulfilling by doing things that many others wouldn't do. I've always told you not to think of your current phase of your life as your best phase. Each phase of life has something unique, and I've learned to live in the moment.

Manisha:
How do you feel about getting older without your sister?

Nalini:
My sister, Niru, and I were never really playmates, but we had a very deep emotional bond. We could talk to each other about anything. Once a week we took long walks and

talked freely with each other. On one of our long walks, we talked about statistics that show that women live longer than men. She said, "If both our husbands die first, we will live together. If we lose some of our senses, we can't lose the same ones at the same time so we will be able to work together as one complete human being." But obviously, that can't be. She departed too early in life. However, I always feel like she is with me. Her guidance makes me strong every day. When I have difficulties taking care of my mother alone, I feel like the guiding force of my sister helps me get through that phase.

Manisha:
Ishani [Manisha's daughter] said that I am most like you. I agreed with her. What do you think?

Nalini:
Ishani is very perceptive and correct. You resemble your dad physically, but your inner workings are just like me, and they were even from an early age. Your clear thinking, ability to plan and think ahead, organizational skills, and courage to do things earlier than your peers are all qualities within me as well. You even got married earlier than your peers! During your teenage years, we had conflicts as all mothers and daughters do. But we were able to overcome our conflicts because we had rapport with each other and saw each other's perspectives.

Interview III: Kapila

Kapila and Hrishi with Piya and Kush

I n 1997, during her freshman year at Yale University, my daughter Kapila had an assignment in her women's studies class to write a biography. She interviewed me, asking poignant questions that encouraged me to give her not just the factual material but also the emotions that were woven into it. She encouraged me to share the details of my significant relationships. As I walked down memory lane, I realized that recalling the people who had influenced my life was touching, pleasurable, and cathartic. She utilized the content of that interview to write her essay for the class.

With her permission, I want to share her essay, which starts from 1946, the year I was born, and provides a summary of the time from that year to the present. In this essay, she describes the many ways that I have constructed my own identity and destiny, bucking tradition and cultural norms. She describes the many moments in my life in which I have been an "uncompromising activist," as my friend Lester once described me.

Several of the short vignettes that she has described in her essay have been developed into full chapters in this memoir with Kapila's encouragement. This essay, which predated the writing of this book by 15 years, represents a summary of my life. I apologize for some repetition. However, the essay adds new details that give a fuller picture of the experiences that shaped who I am.

Biography

by Kapila Juthani

My mother, Dr. Nalini Juthani (maiden name Ghevaria), was born on January 26, 1946, in Mumbai, India, in the year that India won its independence from Great Britain. She was born into the traditional loving home of her two parents and the extended family on her father's side. Her mother was a twenty-year-old housewife, and her father was a young lawyer. Her birth was the result of thirty-six hours of labor. After such an extended period of labor, the doctors offered them two options. Her parents were faced with the decision of choosing to either decapitate their baby or let her mother die of exhaustion. Directly after her father made the decision to decapitate her if necessary, my mother was born. Throughout her life, she used this story to exemplify and remind her of her instinct for survival. This story continuously reminded her that no matter how hard times were for her; she would be able to learn from her experience and survive.

My mother's only memories of her early childhood revolve around her cherished father. She remembers playing with him late at night, not allowing him to sleep. Her next memory includes her father climbing a tree to pick a flower that she had asked for. Up to the age of five, she was a carefree young child who had an absolute faith in and love for her father.

One day, however, she was traveling in an ambulance, only understanding that her beloved father was sick. She remembers being in his hospital room, and seeing him with numerous tubes in him. Her last memory of her father is of him asking her uncle to buy expensive peaches so that he could feed them to his daughter. Her lasting memory of the occasion is her feeling of being completely adored by her father. The next day, she saw all of the women around her wearing white saris, weeping and mourning. She did not understand why. She was told, and she believed that her father had gone to England to get a higher education, but always had the hope that he would return some day. It was not until her teenage years that she truly understood that her father was dead and would not be coming back.

After this event, my mother moved from her father's family's home to the home of her mother's parents. She began to become very close to her maternal grandmother. While her mother was her primary disciplinarian, her grandmother was her nurturer. She looked to her for advice, guidance, and comfort. Her grandmother became her mentor and role model in her personal life, showing her by example how to deal with other people and how to keep her personality balanced.

Approximately six months after her father had died, her baby sister, Niru, was born. Surrounding the birth of this baby girl was an extreme sense of sadness, instead of the expected joy and celebration. Niru grew into a docile, withdrawn, and delicate little girl, and my mother felt the need to always protect her. She became a watchdog, protecting her sister and her mother against cousins and adults whom she perceived as threatening their survival.

In the absence of her father, my mother took on the role of the traditionally male protector in the family, leaving her childhood behind. As a result of her father's death, she became untraditionally assertive, decisive, organized, and determined. One of her aunts once told her that if someone had just heard her speak, they would not have been able to differentiate her from her father. She had developed many of her father's characteristics in his absence. In her home, she became very close to her uncle, who was only fifteen years older than she. She spent a lot of time with him, and began to enjoy playing sports, like boys. Within the household, she served a role similar to her uncle's, engaging in physical activities usually reserved for boys, like carrying heavy items.

When she was between the ages of twelve and sixteen, my mother decided that she wanted to become a doctor. She knew that her father had originally wanted to be a doctor; he had been in a pre-medical college and had had an accident in the lab. As a result, his father, who was a lawyer, took him out of his pre-medical college and sent him to law school. My mother decided that she would carry out the dreams that her father had never been able to. She decided that if she could eventually save the life of one father, for one little girl like herself, all of her hard work would be worthwhile.

My mother's adolescent years were the most tumultuous and difficult years of her life. At that point in her life, she really felt the absence of her father. She felt that his absence was the cause of her insecure feelings. She thought that if he had been there, he would have protected her and taken care of her. During those years, she was torn between the two facets of her personality: she was at once an assertive, quick-thinking, reasoning, academically strong young woman and a vulnerable, insecure little girl. She quickly became tearful and remembers often crying in isolation. While she enjoyed the responsibility of being the oldest child and protector of her family, the child in her often felt completely overwhelmed.

Throughout her adolescent years, my mother received mixed feedback from her family. Most of her male relatives were not happy to see her developing assertiveness and determination. However, while her mother always encouraged her education, she felt that my mother should be trained to fit into a traditional woman's role as well. She thought that if my mother was not obedient and submissive, and well-versed in household duties, such as cooking and cleaning, she would not be able to find a husband. Within her traditional community in India, from the time a daughter was born, finding a husband for her was her family's primary goal. In addition, daughters who did not find husbands ended up as burdens to their families and society.

Therefore, from my grandmother's perspective, the only option for my mother was marriage, which seemed to exclude her career pursuits. However, my mother never succumbed to making a choice between a career and marriage. She knew that she wanted a career and also wanted to get married, and she trusted that things would work out for the best. She believed, as she had always believed, that things in her life would happen for the best, and she would survive through every circumstance. She continued to pursue her career, trusting that at the right time, she would be able to get married and eventually have children. However, she always felt resentful that she was forced to make a choice between becoming a homemaker or a provider. She wished that she could do both.

My mother always respected and loved her mother, but also always knew that she never wanted to be like her.

Her mother's advice to succumb to the traditions showed her that her mother had been a victim of the standards of womanhood in Indian society. She saw her mother feeling like a victim, always at the mercy of everyone else. Her mother was very quickly hurt and brought to tears, and would constantly bring up her past misfortunes as an excuse for problems in her life.

My mother resented the stereotypical role her mother played and also resented the Indian society that put her in that position. She hated the society that forced her mother to give up her own parents after marriage and accept the parents of her husband. She hated the same society that forced her mother to return to her parents when her husband died, forcing her to constantly feel like a burden to her family. My mother hated the traditions that made it unacceptable and unthinkable for a widow, like her mother, to live alone or to remarry.

My mother decided that she would never be a victim as her mother was. She was going to take her life into her own hands and make the things that she wanted happen. Throughout her life, she has taken credit for the good things that have happened and blame for the bad things. However, she always learned from her mistakes, in order to not make them again. She decided to never dwell on the past, finding excuses for her problems. Rather, she would acknowledge them and find solutions. She also decided that she was never going to live dependent on anyone else, simply because she was a woman. She was going to become a doctor, support herself, her mother and her sister, and eventually move to America, where there were many more opportunities.

My mother's disgust with many Indian traditions regarding the position of women, as well as her break with the role that she saw her mother play, put her in a separate category in the eyes of her family. Within her family and society, she was an oddball: one who did not fit in with the traditional role for women in that society. However, because she was considered to be outside the norm, she wasn't restricted by those cultural norms and was able to do the things that she wanted to do in her life. She wasn't judged by the same standards as most women were, and therefore she was able to become a doctor and not spend her days just learning to be a good housewife.

Throughout her early life, my mother had a few very close girlfriends. Her best friend, Amta, was her confidante and companion from elementary school through the present. They looked to each other for companionship, advice, and fun. Amta never obtained a higher education after two years of college but always rejoiced in my mother's academic and career successes. She always supported my mother in all of her endeavors, even though she couldn't truly share in them. In turn, my mother served as Amta's greatest confidante and always listened to her problems. She was always the one that Amta turned to when trying to find solutions to her problems. Despite the distance between them in the past twenty-seven years, with my mother in America and Amta in India, their friendship and mutual respect and companionship has remained.

When my mother entered her highly ranked medical school, she was surprised to find an equal number of women and men in her class. However, many of the men in her class always said that although there were a large number of women enrolled in the medical school, most of them would not actually practice medicine. They said that most of these women were simply in medical school in order to marry a doctor and were therefore taking away the seats of many qualified men. Throughout her life, my mother came across this stereotyped view that women's only goal and function was to get married and be a good housewife. However, regardless of how many times she heard this, she was determined to fight this stereotype.

My mother always knew that she wanted to eventually get married, but there were many things about the institution of marriage in Indian society that she deeply disliked. She found the notion of a dowry completely unacceptable. She did not believe in the necessity of a woman's parents presenting numerous material items to the man's family, practically having the couple's house prepared, as a prerequisite for any marriage for their daughter. She hated the idea that a woman's family would have to literally pay the man's family in order to ensure their daughter's security. My mother found this tradition so distasteful that she would not hesitate to be alone to prevent it.

However, at the age of twenty-four, my mother did get married, an arranged marriage planned by her aunt. My mother and father were initially introduced by members of their respective families, but unlike traditional arranged marriages, they met, got to know each other, and decided whether they wanted to get married. Immediately, my mother found that this man would treat her as an equal partner in their marriage. She saw that he cared for and respected her as a person, not just as a woman. He respected her nurturing qualities but also respected her ambition and higher education. She recognized that this man was very unusual in India, and after approximately a month of knowing each other, they were married. Directly after their marriage, they left India and all of their relatives and friends to come to America.

Not knowing anyone in this strange land, my mother and her new husband arrived in Highland Park, Michigan, where her husband already had a job as a doctor and hospital housing. When she arrived, she had no knowledge of the race tensions that existed in America during the late 1960s and early 1970s. However, during her first few months in America, she found that the hierarchical differences she had felt between men and women in India were reenacted in race in America. In addition, she found that in America, racial divisions only included Caucasians and African-Americans, and she fell into the category of "other." She has therefore spent much of her time and energy, since coming to America, developing her roots and preserving her Indian culture in America.

My mother's first friend in America was a black woman, Cora, with whom she worked. My mother greatly admired her new friend, who had taken care of herself for the majority of her life. After high school, Cora had supported herself through college, and had even worked for a master's degree in education. She lived alone and was not dependent on anyone. My mother was proud to be friends with this woman, who proved that a woman who was determined to set her own path could do whatever was necessary to do that. From Cora, she learned many lessons about how to live and survive in the United States. She learned how to be self-sufficient and do what she needed to do.

For her first five years in America, my mother feels that she was playing the stereotypical role of the ideal woman and wife. Although she had graduated from medical school in India, she worked in many para-medical jobs during her first years in this new country. She spent much of the time completing requirements of internship in India, getting her credentials in order by passing the exams necessary to get residency training in America. Furthermore, she worked to set up a home for herself and her husband and to help her husband establish himself professionally. She felt that in the initial years she had made her ambition and career goals secondary to her husband's. When her first daughter (my older sister) was about one and a half years old, my mother began her residency training in psychiatry. With a great deal of determination and her husband's invaluable help, my mother was able to successfully complete her training. After her four years of residency, she was offered a position as the director of psychiatric education at Bronx Lebanon Hospital. It was a position that had rarely been offered to or held by a woman of color who had graduated from a medical school abroad.

In this position, she went to many faculty meetings in which she was one of only two or three women, and one of the only minorities present. For many years, she felt completely bypassed and overlooked by her white male colleagues at these meetings. She went to similar meetings for over ten years, trying to survive in what she considered an "old boys' club." However, as an astute observer and listener in these meetings, she was able to eventually form personal relationships within that old boys' club. She eventually received the respect of the same men who she felt had ignored her. As she became more confident in her position in her field, she became less self-conscious, which made it easier to feel more equal with her male colleagues. Through the years in her profession, my mother has mentored students, trainees, and young women, whom she could advise.

Although she greatly enjoyed her professional growth and successes, she always considered her family as her first priority. Despite the fact that for many years my mother worked very hard to be a "superwoman," she knew that in the end, raising her three children was most important to her. In addition, she learned that she didn't need to be a superwoman, as her husband would gladly share in both the household and parenting responsibilities. She was a nurturing and ambitious disciplinarian with her children and tried to instill values in her children, such as freedom of thought and speech, courage to become who you want to become, and having a vision and an organized plan.

With me and my older sister, she always tried to instill the belief that we could easily handle a career as well as a family. She showed us, through her example, that not only was it possible, but it was very fulfilling as well. In addition, she was very quick to correct us when we played role-playing games, putting ourselves in traditionally female career positions. We did not have to limit ourselves to being nurses or teachers; we had the opportunity to do whatever we wanted to. She did not want us to be influenced by the societal assumptions about gendered professional roles.

She feels that her parenting has been one of the most important responsibilities in her life. She feels that seeing her children with the values she worked so hard to instill in them makes all of her efforts worthwhile. This is how she has always looked at her life: her achievements make her frustrations worthwhile.

Throughout her life, my mother faced many trying and frustrating times, but she used her experiences to learn lessons for the future. As she learned from the story about her birth, she knew that she would always find a way to survive and continue working toward her goals. She found power in her failures and misfortunes and was able to turn them to her benefit. This has been her philosophy and attitude about her life, and she has used it to be content and in control of her destiny.

Nalini and Viren's family at Viral and Rupa's wedding

Edwards Brothers Malloy
Oxnard, CA USA
August 21, 2013